Christine Hausmann

Bending tradition to the changing times

Christine Hausmann

Bending tradition to the changing times

The use of video as an empowerment tool in
nonformal adult education in Zimbabwe

IKO – Verlag für Interkulturelle Kommunikation

Bibliographische Information der Deutschen Bibliothek
Die Deutsche Bibliothek verzeichnet diese Publikation in der Deutschen
Nationalbibliographie; detaillierte bibliographische Daten sind im Internet über
http://dnb.ddb.de abrufbar.

©   IKO-Verlag für Interkulturelle Kommunikation
      Frankfurt am Main • London, 2004

      Frankfurt am Main   London
      Postfach 90 04 21   70 c, Wrentham Avenue
      D - 60444 Frankfurt   London NW10 3HG, UK

      e-mail: info@iko-verlag.de • Internet: www.iko-verlag.de

      ISBN: 3-88939-732-8

Umschlaggestaltung: Volker Loschek, 61184 Karben
Herstellung: Bookstation GmbH, 78244 Gottmadingen

Table of contents

3

List of graphs, tables and charts

Preface and acknowledgements

From continuous research in the field of nonformal education for empowerment it transpires that a fruitful approach to 'gendered'[1] issues in education is connected to the understanding that women's issues are inseparable from men's issues. Any approach to women's empowerment through education without considering women's husbands, sons, brothers or fathers - men - seems especially in the Zimbabwean context doomed to fail. It is believed that development can occur through facilitating people's access to information. This view suggests the support of creative environments by supplying *different people with different needs* with information to make their informed choices. Measures and strategies in the process of information transmission should however bear in mind that due to the triple burden, women are more disadvantaged in different spheres of life especially when it comes to information access. It is assumed that practices of especially Shona (mainly Zezuru) culture, which is explored in this thesis, are influenced by life-style, area of residence, family background and ac-

---

[1]'Gender' can be defined as socially ascribed meanings given to the categories 'man' and 'woman'. It refers to widely shared ideas and norms about men and women. 'Gender' is opposed to 'sex', which refers to male and female biological attributes (De Bruyn 1995: 12). According to Stromquist (1999: 5), three meanings of 'gender' are currently discussed: The first refers to unequal relations between men and women that create problems and disadvantages for women, the second deals with questioning the way men are socialised, assuming dominant roles and the third meaning focuses also on men and how they suffer (but, according to Stromquist, thereby disregarding the fact that men are responsible for the subordination of women). The view supported in this study has a bit of each, accepting that unequal relations cause disadvantages for some women, but also for some men. That men are not always to be blamed for women's disadvantages is explained through the second meaning, which points out a crucial aspect that needs more attention and thorough research. It is further accepted that some men are suffering within their assumed roles and the expectations these roles carry. However, the view supported in this study looks at women and men in their own right, it tries to respect the different needs of both and intends to bring both together for dialogue.

7

cess to education and information. These practices are part of lived realities of different individuals and groups.

It should furthermore be pointed out that what is provided in this study is a personal choice of data, interpreted in a manner that is influenced by the author's personal background - beyond doubt these findings are 'coloured' by the author's own reality and shaped by her own experience. To say it with Walker's (1990: 7) words:

"This is not to claim, that (..) I (my adding) have a monopoly on either the material or the analysis, nor to deny the need for and the importance of the academic work of those who (...) are 'closer in terms of culture, language, class, race and gender' to the lived experience of black women in this region".

This study would not have been possible without the tremendous support and patience of individuals and communities throughout Zimbabwe and Germany.

Mr. John Riber, the director of Media for Development Trust (MFD) in Zimbabwe, has provided the idea for the project and has constantly encouraged and supported it for the past four years. The *Neria* materials described in this study are available at Media for Development Trust, mfdadmin@mango.zw, 19 Van Praagh Ave, Milton Park, P.O. Box 6755, Harare, Zimbabwe.

Generous financial assistance from the Swedish International Development Corporation Agency (Sida), as well as the Department for International Development Central Africa (DfID) facilitated the implementation of projects this study is based upon.

Mr. Titus Moetsabi, managing agent of the Wills and Inheritance Laws Programme, now country co-ordinator of the Academy for Educational Development (AED)'s SMART Work Programme in Zimbabwe has been an important discussion partner during and beyond the programme.

Last but not least, my parents, Erika and Peter Hausmann, have supported the idea from the start - without them it would have not been possible to pursue this challenging goal.

Executive summary

"Legal rights education is not just passing on information about laws or procedures. It must lead to a critical awareness of the law. This implies that legal rights education must go beyond the letters of the law but lead to an understanding and appreciation of the fundamental social values reflected in the law. It is only when women and communities can identify with those values or with the reasoning behind the law that change in their attitudes and practices is possible" (Agimbe et al 1994: 5).

This study examines the empowering effects of film and video among participants of various nonformal adult education programmes and initiatives in Zimbabwe. Specifically, it investigates the impact of the locally made educating and entertaining feature film, *Neria*, and its educational supporting material, on four dimensions of empowerment namely, cognitive, emotional, political and economic. The findings are based mainly on participants' short-term and subjective experience of change in these dimensions. Data that led to these findings was gathered during film screenings and focus group discussions with 27 non-governmental organisations (NGOs), during key informant interviews as well as through 1244 questionnaires completed by female and male road show screening participants in rural, peri-urban and urban areas on the one hand and female-only Ladies' Clubs' members in urban high-density areas on the other.

Educational material for *Neria* has been developed during the *Neria* Grassroots Distribution Project, which aimed at increasing discussion about the new Laws of Inheritance, but focused further on the demonstration of inheritance-related problems faced mainly by widows and children. This audio-visual support material included a support video, focusing on the key learning points contained in the feature film, *Neria*, and a support manual to facilitate a guided discussion process of target beneficiaries. To reach, especially, disadvantaged groups across Zimbabwe, the material has first been distributed to the grassroots, utilising a network of NGO's and institutions throughout the country and has then been utilised in a nation-wide multimedia educational awareness campaign, initiated by the Zimbabwean Ministry of Justice, Legal and Parliamentary Affairs.

By exploring causes and effects, the study succeeds in showing that *Neria*, together with its supporting material, which was developed in consultation with the intended beneficiaries, assists in empowering the individual, especially at a cognitive and emotional level.

A strong awareness of a number of inheritance laws, as well as strategies to deal with gender inequalities in family and society has been created, knowledge has been increased and levels of self-confidence have been raised. As interactive tools, the designed material has proved to encourage awareness among audiences on the issue of women's rights, and has moved communities to respond and build on existing initiatives for attitude and behavioural change. Male participants have clearly indicated the strong intention and commitment to change their habits by writing wills, while women have learnt that they do not have to comply with oppressive tradition and have to speak out to break the silence. They have further learnt to question existing negative attitudes.

The idea of group formation - through perceiving the need to discuss inheritance-related issues with like-minded individuals, as well as through perceiving the advantage of being economically independent from the spouse, by implementing joint income-generation activities, as in *Neria* - has been clearly strengthened, which can support political and economic empowerment.

Through the special learning environments in which the material was used, it could be further shown that the knowledge gained through understanding inheritance-related messages was much more sustainable when the film and its messages were discussed in a focus group, as was practised in the Ladies' Clubs.

However, as far as concrete knowledge about the content of the Laws of Inheritance as well as procedures to access inheritance benefits are concerned, the material needs to be utilised in combination with other tools, to ensure that all necessary information reaches the disadvantaged, and people are empowered in a sustainable manner.

Long-term insights, which could be gathered from some participants, suggest that, although *Neria* empowers, the infrastructure one needs to utilise to counter inheritance-related problems is either not available or not effective enough. While the *Neria* material has managed to convince, especially, women that it is possible to succeed by making use of the formal legal system - taking the matter to court or engaging a lawyer - once abuse has occurred, the harsh reality of long waiting periods or ineffective support structures can be discouraging.

The study highlights that it will take some time and repetition of the programme to have a lasting impact especially on rural decision makers. Apart from restructuring the formal legal system and extending it to the rural and peri-urban areas of Zimbabwe, it is suggested that more supportive programmes are implemented. The stress death causes for those left behind, the hardships faced when being overruled, and the threats that have to be endured when standing up against the extended family, are so immense that counselling needs to be a crucial component of those programmes.

What becomes so clear is that all aspects of inheritance will continue to be priority issues for Zimbabweans, not only due to the HIV/AIDS pandemic, but also due to a rapid change of societal patterns and values. This justifies the call for a continuous and thorough discussion of inheritance-related issues in programmes that aim at empowering Zimbabweans, in general, and the disadvantaged, in particular. Video, it is recommended, should be a favoured alternative tool in adult education and a qualitative method of further research that investigates ways of strengthening the status of women and empowering its beneficiaries to make informed choices throughout their lives.

Introduction

The use of audio-visual media in nonformal adult education in the context of international development co-operation has been known as an effective method for years. More and more, local films and videos are also being used for a variety of education and training purposes.

How specifically locally produced educational films and videos can have effects on their viewers and which reactions they can trigger, as far as the Southern African region is concerned, however, not often been at the core of thorough research. This is particularly true for films and videos that are designed to entertain and educate at the same time. As a result, the potential of film and video as an agent of attitudinal and behavioural change is - especially in the field of gender, empowerment and development - therefore rather underrated.

The following study is designed to contribute to a stronger focus on the potential of films and videos in adult education. Building onto a theory of empowerment in the field of nonformal adult education, the example of a frequently used film in the field of gender, empowerment and legal education in Zimbabwe should assist to highlight the manifold areas in which film and video can be used in nonformal adult education. How this medium can moreover facilitate outstanding learning processes, how it can change attitudes in favour of the improvement of women's status in a sustainable manner and how it can trigger thereby empowerment processes, should be shown in the course of this study.

This should be achieved being guided by the following seven main research questions:

1. What are the contexts of the use of the entertainment education film *Neria* in Zimbabwe and what activities accompany the film screening?
2. What are viewers' attitudes towards and opinions about the film *Neria*? What are experiences of trainers?
3. What are awareness levels, attitudes, practices and knowledge of formal and informal inheritance-related processes amongst rural and urban-based intended programme beneficiaries in Zimbabwe and how can educational audio-visual support material that acknowledges these indigenous resources be developed?

13

4. Are change processes triggered through the use of the material? If so, of what nature are these?

5. How does discussion and learning group composition contribute to the film's impact?

6. What are lessons learnt and challenges experienced in the development and distribution process of entertainment educational audio-visual material in Zimbabwe?

7. How can entertainment educational films and videos in general contribute to a 'bottom up - empowerment' in development co-operation?

While Chapter 1 should serve mainly to outline the background theories utilised in this study, Chapter 2 will provide socio-cultural background information on the practices and laws of inheritance in Zimbabwe and will explore the empowerment needs of women and communities with respect to inheritance. It will be of great interest to see how film/video in general - and the locally produced message film *Neria* in particular - has been utilised in nonformal education in Zimbabwe so far. This will be observed after supplying information on theories and practices of film/video as tools for attitude and behaviour change in adult education for empowerment in Zimbabwe in Chapter 3. Chapter 4 will explore participative strategies for the design and development of training material based on *Neria* by describing processes and experiences of the *Neria* Grassroots Distribution Project. The further distribution of this training material within a multimedia educational awareness campaign, the Wills and Inheritance Laws Programme of the Zimbabwean Ministry of Justice will be observed afterwards. Chapter 5 will then specifically analyse the feedback of target beneficiaries towards this communication material utilised in three different learning environments. Finally, in Chapter 6, the analysis will be transferred to the dimensions of empowerment and will observe how far and at which levels target groups could be empowered. How effective and sustainable film and video empowerment tools aimed at improving women's legal status should be designed and how external conditions need to be adapted to sustain this improvement will be explored in conclusion.

0. Research methodology

Data for this research project has been gathered between October 1998 and October 2002 in Zimbabwe. In the course of two development co-operation projects, the manifold effects of an entertainment education video on potential target groups have been observed.

0.1 Theories applied

The data collection and analysis exercise was characterised by *grounded theory*, which Weis Bentzon et al (1998) define as an

"iterative process in which data and theory, lived reality and perceptions about norms are constantly engaged with each other to help the researcher decide what data to collect and how to interpret it. The interaction between developing theories and methodology is constant, as preliminary assumptions direct the data collection and then the collected data, when analysed, indicates new directions and new sources of data" (18).

This refers, according to Glaser and Strauss (1967) to the discovery of theory from data obtained in a systematic way from social research as well as to the use of comparative analysis as a strategy to develop new theories. In this view, theory is emphasised as process and a constantly developing item as opposed to a perfected product[2]. Grounded theory or theories can be discovered by reconstructing *meaning patterns*[3] through *thick description*. Easton (1997: 163f) describes thick description as

"information on phenomena and events that includes not only richly detailed perceptions of their characteristics but also to a good deal about their context and history,

---

[2] Glaser and Strauss (1967: 6) suggest that when generating theory from the data, hypotheses and concepts stem from the data and are at the same time systematically worked out in relation to that data over the course of the research.

[3] Meaning patterns then are configurations that will decide how experience will be interpreted and placed in categories. Information will be configured in patterns in human brains that help remember things or evaluate new experiences. These patterns do furthermore reveal priorities, a value system or problem solving devices. They define situations as well as they are guided by norms of behaviour. However, these meaning patterns do usually only become visible if they are violated or put into question (Easton 1997: 168).

about how the people most affected experience and view them, about what other things seem most closely associated with them".

Six tools are important guidelines in a grounded research process[4]. Following these, this research can be regarded as grounded in the sense that there was a constant search for additional ideas, materials and methods beyond those initially identified. Each data gathering exercise opened up new ways of exploration; a rich in-depth data-gathering process that led to qualitative insights into different types of people's matters of concern. A critical data analysis was usually conducted after each data-gathering phase to highlight how far the data could contribute to a theory development and how far results could be generalised.

0.2 Data gathering steps

While, originally, the data gathering process for this study focused on the material development phase, it was soon extended to the dissemination of this material under different conditions – small-scale (distributors) and large-scale (campaign) and the audience's perception of and their reaction to these developed materials.

0.2.1 Preparation phase

Using mainly semi-structured interviews with 15 resource persons from 12 NGOs and 35 individuals in Zimbabwe, an attempt was made to find out

---

[4] An open mind (being aware of basic assumptions and its basis), next question technique (data collection and theory building are parallel processes, which means, by analysing earlier gathered data, results lead to new questions and fields to be explored), concept building (refers to the gradual build up of the data and observations on the data and the need to review critical concepts), constant comparative method (ongoing comparison of data), theoretical selection or sampling (beyond expanding particular predetermined data into expanding the research's goal; a process where one decides on analytical grounds what data to collect next), limitations on theory building (review of the development of suppositions, models and theories; testing of results under the guiding question: Do the theories adequately address concrete problems encountered in the field and uttered by individuals?) (see Weis Bentzon et al 1998: 178-188).

more about the popularity of the film *Neria*, its use in a variety of education and training programmes, people's attitudes towards the film and their reactions after seeing the film. Existing literature on theories and on studies of similar subjects were considered.

0.2.2 First field phase

Screenings and focus group discussions were carried out between August and October 2000. A total of 27 out of 30 distributors' groups were visited throughout Zimbabwe. During 27 screenings, a total of 953 participants and staff members held focus group discussions to give comments on issues of relevance to the project. A total of 20 identified key persons then later participated in in-depth interviews. Screenings were held in towns (high-density areas) with rural and urban participants as well as in remote areas, at a particular growth point or training centre with selected rural participants from all the district(s) around. The composition of the groups was in most cases manifold, covering a vast age range, both sexes and a variety of occupations. Group sizes varied from 10 to 130.

The screening and discussions took, in most cases, approximately three hours, but were extended up to a full day, where participants had travelled from far or where screenings were carried out in remote areas. In most cases, the screening was incorporated into a workshop or meeting, where the researcher and/or the resident trainer or group leader was given three hours or more to introduce her or himself, explain thoroughly about the project, screen the film and start the discussion. Usually, people started to discuss immediately about issues of relevance brought up in *Neria*. The comments were recorded and later transcribed by two local research assistants. While these transcripts were reviewed, special focus was on stories, accounts, and experiences to provide insight into empowering and disempowering dimensions of women and men's communication. The gathered data was analysed inductively to give respect to the most common subjects triggered by the viewing of the film. Key words, phrases and themes were clustered and incorporated into a draft format of the support video as well as the manual. These drafts were circulated amongst NGO representatives, members of the design team, independent consultants and members of the public. Comments and suggestions were included in the drafts.

0.2.3 Second field phase

The second field phase aimed at pre-testing the communication material. Potential target groups from urban, semi-urban and rural areas tested the video and parts of the support manual in English, Shona and Ndebele. The tests were carried out with distributors' groups, different from those who had participated in the original *Neria* screenings. In most cases, participants were divided into six subgroups to discuss the six sequences of the manual in combination with the video. Groups returned to the plenary after a certain time and reported back on their findings. A local facilitator probed answers from the groups and moderated the discussion. Sessions took, in most cases, two to three hours. Additionally, 20 key informant interviews were carried out to supplement the information needed for the final design of the material. Of these, 15 were held with women and five with men. From March through to May 2001, a total of 449 people participated in 11 pre-testing sessions. Their impressions, ideas and recommendations were incorporated into the draft material.

NGO networks and institutions that later used the material, provided evaluation and project progress reports of their programmes and informed about how the material was used with which results. Out of 30 groups who had participated in the project, 17 groups provided this feedback six months to one year after the implementation of the project.

0.2.4 Third field phase

The third field phase served to investigate reactions of target beneficiaries to the material through an evaluation questionnaire handed out during the information campaign of the Zimbabwean Ministry of Justice, Legal and Parliamentary Affairs. In the course of this programme, the *Neria* video was screened 196 times during road shows (140 rural and 56 urban) and 448 times with Ladies' Clubs (four sessions a week in four provinces between May and November 2002). 93 road show screenings (59 rural and 34 urban) and 60 Ladies' Clubs' screenings and programmes were part of the research carried out for this study. Programme participants (or road show crew on behalf of participants) completed 12 evaluation forms per Ladies' Clubs' session and a maximum of six forms per road show session. Team leaders of Ladies' Clubs organised their own screenings and completed their forms; all of which were collected at the end of a five months' tour (May to September 2002).

The audience of road shows comprised children, youngsters, adults as well as the elderly. 26-45 year old participants were in the majority. As far as total audience numbers are concerned, a total of 352 600 road show viewers and 15 597 Ladies' Clubs' viewers could be counted throughout Zimbabwe from May to September 2002. However, while a total of 352 600 road show viewers and 3 498 Ladies' Clubs' viewers were present when the research was carried out, feedback was gained from a random[5] selection of 524 road show viewers (248 female and 276 male participants) and 720 Ladies' Clubs' members (female only). Their responses were translated and in case of unclear information, were discussed with the research assistants. This study utilises data and results gathered from 1998 through to 2002[6].

0.3   Data gathering techniques

Focus group discussions produced a wealth of data on issues of concern to this study. They were supplemented by *semi-structured interviews* and *in-depth interviews*. *Key informants* in this process were police officers, judges, lawyers, social workers, nurses, paralegals, NGO staff, teachers, trainers, chiefs and traditional healers as well as widows or widowers, who were interviewed to obtain data, opinions and perspectives on a topic, which led to new key persons and subjects. Open questions prevailed. The *observation of participants* when interacting with their society, their fami-

---

[5] Road show crewmembers and Ladies' Clubs' personnel chose a variety of participants every day. It was attempted to choose people from 25 up to 60 years to reduce the number of spoilt forms obtained from very young participants earlier on.

[6] For ideas on residential areas of all research participants, see Appendix 2.1 and 2.2.

19

lies or officials also helped to explore why some activities took place the way they did and which factors influence the behaviour and attitude of people[7]. The *questionnaires* for distributors as well as the *informal survey* for target beneficiaries and audience members did produce quantitative data, but differed from sample surveys by focusing on a few variables, a small number of questions and on a small sample. The sampling process was done by convenience in order to reach participants where they were easily accessible.

All interviews with officials were held in English, while group discussions, in-depth interviews as well as the questionnaire exercise were conducted in vernacular languages and were translated by either the respective facilitator of the screening, by research assistants or staff of the University of Zimbabwe.

Graph 1 below summarises the research statistics. A total of 23 in-depth interviews with 41 people were conducted between 1998 and 2002. Of these, 25 were women and 16 were men. While for the preliminary study, only one woman was interviewed, 20 people were interviewed in the process of the material development (nine women and 11 men) and 20 people during the pre-testing. Of these, 15 were women and five were men. As far as screenings in combination with focus group discussions are concerned, a total of 43 screenings with 1 430 people were conducted between 1998 and 2002. Of these, 706 were women and 724 were men. During the phase of the preliminary study, 35 people (28 women and seven men) watched and discussed the film, while during the phase of material development, 956 people (416 women and 540 men) participated in the programme. Pre-testing involved a total of 449 people (257 women and 192 men).

---

[7] This is based on the assumption that relations between individuals, gender hierarchies and power structures can, when being observed systematically for some time, help to unveil practices and reasons that hinder an empowerment thought.

20

Graph 1 – Research tools 1998-2002

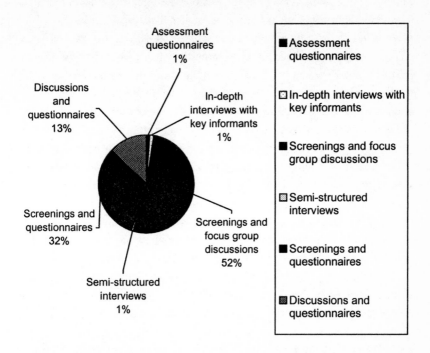

As far as semi-structured interviews are concerned, these were carried out 12 times with 15 people (eight women and seven men) in the phase of the preliminary study only. Screenings in combination with questionnaires were conducted with 884 road shows and Ladies' Clubs' members (608 women and 276 men), while another group of 360 Ladies' Clubs' members discussed the topic of the film only and completed the questionnaires later.

The attitude change analysis focuses on the material development and distribution phase only. Preliminary study results are only quoted to support insights gained from the other data. While qualitative data (see also Friebertshaeuser, Prengel 1997) clearly prevailed in this study, quantitative data collected through the questionnaires and with focus groups was mainly used to illustrate trends in numbers.

0.4 Some thoughts about the data gathering exercise

Much has been written about the necessity, when gathering data in Africa, to critically question data gathering techniques that have been developed in a Western context. Some authors go as far as suggesting that results from qualitative research and answers from participants, gathered in the course of interviews, are usually flawed, assuming that participants provide what has been called a 'fügsame Antwort' (an obedient reply) (Durt 1992: 184); being part of the 'conspiracy of courtesy' (Anyaegbunam et al 1998: 48, see also Fetterman 1994). Given that age and status factors are not neglected, experience shows that Shona people do voice their opinions freely when talking to a person or group they know. In this study, this was considered by making use of already established networks, community gatherings and meetings, into which the data gathering exercise could be easily incorporated. Instructed trainers from NGOs who knew their target groups well, usually carried out the task. Where information was in Shona or Ndebele respectively, it was recorded and translated by the research assistants. When conducting their discussion, people very soon ignored the researcher's presence and voiced criticism freely as their discussions cored around the film and the community's lived customs.

This differed, however, when the road shows questionnaire exercise was carried out. Although the crew was trained, people did not seem to see the importance of accuracy when recording data. The political climate furthermore prohibited repeating some data gathering exercises as well as validating results in the field. These points need to be kept in mind when judging findings of this study.

Chapter I
Applied theories

1 Empowerment

Empowerment has become a so-called buzzword in so many different fields of study and has been influenced by all these different fields somehow, so that the attempt to provide an overview, let alone a definition, becomes a hard task. The concept has manifold connotations, and therefore needs to be adjusted to the object of study in a certain cultural and social context. In the following, an overview of empowerment ideas, with a specific focus on the educational field, will be provided.

1.1 Definition - the different notions of empowerment

What most definitions have in common is the idea that empowerment marks a *process* which is aimed at maintaining or changing the nature and distribution of power in a particular cultural context through action (Bookman, Morgen 1988: 4). Power, closely connected to the word, is in this sense being understood as a resource, as the ability to motivate and transform the given, as the ability to change things in any social context. Power expresses the consolidation of transforming and creative abilities and is constituted of social, material and intellectual wealth. It can be understood as a basis for social status (see also McFadden 1997).

While some consider that empowerment is often linked with an individual's sense of confidence, many authors stress the importance of seeing it more in a holistic sense (see Dighe 1995). White and Nair (1999: 49) for example, define empowerment as the outcome of establishing and strengthening interpersonal commitment and trust. Alliances of groups of diverse individuals share a similar sense of helplessness and lack of control.

In the context of education, empowerment can be

"learning through collective action that they can successfully challenge individuals and institutions opposed to their self-interests" (Papanek 1990 in Stein 1997: 45).

All the above mentioned aspects reappear in Nelly Stromquist's (1993; 1995, 1997) definition of empowerment as a learning strategy which exceeds goals such as political participation and awareness raising in order to give respect to cognitive, emotional, economic and political components (see below). Learning should positively influence behaviour that ties understanding to a plan of action for the benefit of the rights of, particularly, women (Stromquist 1995: 19).

1.2   Background - the roots of empowerment

The concept of empowerment has its roots mainly in the Civil Rights Movement that took place in the United States of America in the 1960s. Equal voting rights for black citizens should be achieved with a variety of protest activities, aimed at uniting marginalised groups to define and utter their goals and to gain power to support their interests in society. This movement evolved from the Highlander School and its activities[8]. Other influences on the Civil Rights Movement included anti-colonialism activities and popular education. Popular education, a concept promoted by Paulo Freire, had a direct impact on the empowerment movement. His methodology of 'critical consciousness' or 'conscientisation' should give education the role of facilitating critical reflection of life circumstances, allowing learners to be subjects and actors of their own lives[9]. This is based on a philosophy that relies on the faculty of people to understand, learn and act using local resources in a manner that can influence or change history's

---

[8] The Highlander Folk School, founded by Myles Horton in 1932, provided training for people striving for social justice. 'Citizenship Schools' was one of the school's programme. Classes designed to provide literacy training were moulded to 'conscientisation' groups with the goal of community organisation. Highlander can therefore be regarded as the most important influence on the Civil Rights Movement (see Stein 1997: 55).

[9] The main task of this form of adult education is to instigate a process of critical reflection that should lead to action and change (Lind, Johnston 1990: 79). Components of this popular education include active listening, participatory dialogues and critical problem solving of social, economic, political and historic contexts of participants' lives (Freire 1973), see also Adams (1997: 38f) or Walker (1981).

path. It is based on the axiom that a human being's historical vocation is to become free from psychological and material oppression, with liberation being its central goal and revolutionary pedagogy as the means (Scrampickal 1994: 6f; Hochheimer 1999).

Since all movements for social change were aimed at opposing different kinds of oppression, empowerment can be seen as a global concept (Stein 1997: 52). In the 1970s, the empowerment concept re-arose when international attention focused on powerless groups in the context of development theory and practice. The women's movement applied the concept to women in Third World countries, which led to an increased awareness of the disadvantaged situation of women in general. International activists, donor organisations, as well as spontaneous grassroots activities in different countries, all contributed to women's empowerment activities and to what can be called an international women's empowerment movement (Stein 1997: 53, see also Hausmann 1998: 55-56). By now, empowerment is recognised as a basic human right and has been a central policy goal of international conferences[10] (UNFPA 2001).

1.3 Empowerment components

While the dimensions of empowerment are manifold, different researchers find different components of empowerment meaningful. Most authors differentiate between factors that relate to a person and factors that relate to a group. According to Stromquist (1995: 14-15), empowerment is a process that combines consciousness-raising and action (personal and group factors respectively) for individuals to understand society and challenge, at the same time, their position in society in combination with others (Jongepier, Appel 1995: 67). In this view, cognitive, emotional, political and economic components need to interact in order for meaningful empowerment to be achieved. Different skills that address the different components need to be

---

[10] Examples are the Fourth World Conference on Women (FWCW) in Beijing in 1995, the World Summit for Social Development in 1995, the World Food Summit in 1996, Habitat II in 1996, the fifth-year review of ICPD implementation (ICPD+5) in 1999 and the World Education Forum in Dakar in 2002.

transmitted and strengthened in the process. Table 1 below brings together empowerment skills/indicators suggested by Stromquist.

Table 1 – Empowerment skills/indicators

Component	Skill/indicator	Target	Result
Cognitive	- Understanding the self and the need to make choices that might be against cultural and social expectations, - Acquiring new knowledge about sexuality[11] and especially legal rights, - Naming problems and identifying action leading to solutions (Stromquist 1995: 14-15; 1997).	Individual	- Awareness is raised, knowledge is gained, and changed beliefs or opinions are expressed.
Emotional	- Feeling self-confident (to be in a position to act at personal and societal levels), - Believing that one can succeed in one's efforts, - Self-esteem and a positive changed self-image (Stromquist 1995: 14-15; 1997).	Individual, group	- Changed beliefs and feelings are expressed.
Political	- Analysing the environment in political and social terms (individual awareness), - Organising and mobilising for social change (collective action), - Participating in non-family groups (Stromquist 1995: 14-15).	Individual, group	- New behaviour is implemented or behavioural intentions are expressed.
Economic	- Engaging in income generation for economic autonomy (Stromquist 1995: 14-15).	Individual, group	- New behaviour is implemented or behavioural intentions are expressed.

---

[11] The freedom to make reproductive choices supported by knowledge about sexuality is seen by many as a cornerstone of the empowerment process (see UNFPA 1995: 1).

1.3.1 Ways of thinking – the cognitive component

Stromquist (1995) suggests that skills such as the understanding of the self and the need to make choices against cultural and social expectations need to be addressed as part of the cognitive empowerment component. Acquiring new knowledge about sexuality and especially legal rights is also crucial, because

"in most countries, (...) legislation for gender equity and women's rights is well ahead of practice; women therefore need to know which legal rights already exist in order to press for their implementation and enforcement" (14).

The ability to name problems and to identify action that leads to sustainable solutions is a further skill in this respect. Cognitive skills are aimed at raising awareness and strengthening the individual process of gaining knowledge, which should result in expressing changed beliefs or opinions about an issue, a person or an object.

1.3.2 Ways of feeling – the emotional component

Stromquist (1995; 1997) lists the development of a feeling of self-confidence (to be in a position to act at personal and societal levels) and the formation of a belief that a person can succeed in her or his efforts as skills of the emotional component. An increased ability for problem-solving and increased self-esteem or a positive changed self-image should result from the process of strengthening these beliefs. Women should greaten their power by increasing internal strength and self-reliance as opposed to domination. Power is here defined as

"the right to determine one's own choices in life and to influence the direction of change through resource control gain" (Jongepier, Appel 1995: 66).

This is in so far necessary as it is understood that powerless individuals have internalised oppressive beliefs, thinking they deserve to be less powerful than others (Bell 1997: 5).

Emotional empowerment skills deal with positive beliefs and feelings of and about a person towards her or himself and the environment - beliefs that need to be strengthened. They deal with a person's capacity to perceive her or himself first and foremost as an individual and, if possible, to distinguish herself from collective characteristics (women, especially, are often part of a collective identity and do not utter their individual needs). This means a form of differentiation from others, a mobilisation of own capacities (see also Valdez 1999: 84f). As a result, changed feelings and beliefs should be expressed.

1.3.3 Ways of expressing intentions or ways of behaving – the political component

This component is for many authors the most crucial, since it combines all other components when action takes place or behaviour is performed. For Stromquist (1995), this is likely with an increased ability to analyse the environment in political and social terms (what she calls individual awareness) and the ability to organise and mobilise for social change (what she calls collective action). Collective action, especially, is what is usually associated with the political or social dimension of empowerment. The participation[12] in non-family groups is an important indicator of this action.

Empowerment has a strong communicative aspect, mainly based on an interaction process with a person's community. Empowerment has further been explored under behavioural aspects:

"Empowering behaviour refers to the specific actions a person takes to exercise influence on the socio-political environment through participation in community organisations and activities" (Papa et al 2000: 93).

The political component of empowerment deals with inter-group relationships between members of a household, community or society[13]. Specific formations, that group like-minded individuals together to organise for

---

[12]Easton (1997: 30) suggests "Participation denotes initiatives through which people acquire increased and broadened responsibility for decision-making, resource allocation, implementation of activities and assessment of their results in areas of immediate concern to their lives as well as the competence necessary to play these enhanced roles. This includes some degree of actual 'empowerment' and not just token participation".

[13] Most of the authors studied see empowerment tied to the common levels of governance such as household, community and society. According to some authors, the behaviour expected of women in a given cultural group is organised around their three roles at these levels, namely the reproductive role within the household, the productive role within society and the role within the community (Murphy 1995: 23).

28

change (however crucial this change should be and at whichever level of society it should take place) should be created. It is supposed to result in action - the implementation of a new behaviour or the expression of new behavioural intentions.

1.3.4 Ways of expressing intentions or ways of behaving – the economic component

The economic component is linked with some form of action of a person or a group and can therefore also be listed under ways of behaving. Women in particular need their own independent income in order to acquire a sense of decision-making power by earning and using their money according to their needs and desires.

Moreover, the fact that women can contribute in monetary terms towards the household income is perceived to be a facilitator for power negotiations. In times of economic regression and hardships, the income of a woman is well received by men and supports, in many cases, women's further steps outside the house. Economic autonomy is a crucial supportive component; money is usually almost always a strong power factor in family and society. As a result of transmitting these specific empowerment skills, some form of action - the implementation of the new behaviour or at least the expression of new behavioural intentions - should take place.

1.3.5 Combining empowering components

As it transpires from skills and categories discussed above, all components are closely connected. While the provision of knowledge and the training of skills can have effects on the psyche of individuals and can influence their individual or group action, action can also influence the psyche and knowledge of others. As Young (1994) observes, the process of organising for change like networking, sharing responsibilities, or simply talking together, enhances emotional empowerment and facilitates political empowerment. The group aspect is here of considerable importance, since people can derive increased self-confidence when they speak out freely in groups that validate their personal experience. Through collective action, a positive change can be brought about, which can lead to opportunities for knowledge gain, access to resources and a better quality of life (see also UNFPA 2002: 28).

One component cannot function without another and the different aspects need to reflect when empowerment processes are measured. As Chart 1 below shows, all components are interconnected. No linear stages or steps are being followed - rather, the process of gaining understanding of all components should have empowering effects.

Chart 1 – The combination of empowerment components

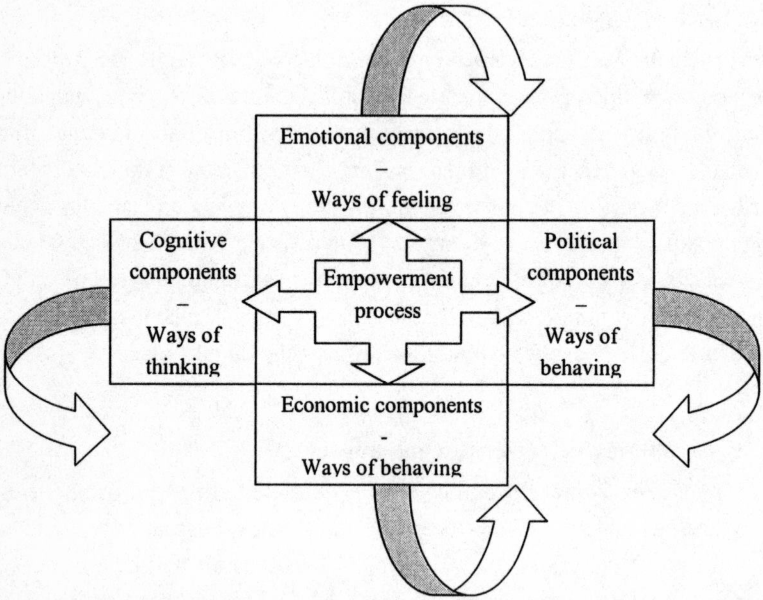

Emotional components

–

Ways of feeling

Cognitive components

–

Ways of thinking

Empowerment process

Political components

–

Ways of behaving

Economic components

-

Ways of behaving

1.4   The goal of empowerment

Empowerment theorists see the strengthening of individual (in most cases, female) capacity, in order to challenge barriers opposed to self-interests, as

30

a main goal of empowerment. According to the radical feminist[14] position of Longwe (1998: 19f), these self-interests are gender issues in a patriarchal society, expressed through gender discrimination in custom, law and ideological belief. According to her, there is a conservative and a radical approach to empowerment; the goal of the former being to equip individuals with skills to advance in the existing society (individual self-reliance), while the latter is aimed at radically restructuring the society. Whichever approach one favours, there is consensus that empowerment is a long-term process with a general goal: a raised consciousness through critical reflection about one's own condition, leading to social action. This action could be aimed at strengthening the disadvantaged in leadership and decision-making, facilitating their access to education, increasing their access to and control over economic resources, supporting their access to health information and control over the own body as well as improving women's self-esteem and their sense of personal power.

Communication is decisive for the empowerment process. Participatory in nature, communication resources should be made accessible to people who learn skills that will enable them to form partnerships with others. This process, so it is believed, can make people aware of social issues relevant to their lives. Individuals will be transformed from a powerless position to the point where they are active communicators expressing choices and decisions that affect their personal and political life (White, Nair 1999: 48f).

As a perception (based on the belief that a person is able to induce activities and people to achieve desired goals without experiencing interference from external forces, and act accordingly) empowerment will depend on the person's belief in her or his communication skills to achieve

---

[14] Feminism consists of a diverse body of related thoughts describing women's encounters with patriarchy, oppression, power as well as the devaluation of female concerns. When exploring feminist perspectives on empowerment, the main underlying rationale identifies that patriarchy exists in most societies and that men's domination over women must end so that women can experience any form of significant empowerment. How exactly measures and strategies to end male domination should be designed depends mainly on different feminist positions (Papa et al 2000: 96).

31

these changes (Papa et al 1997: 6ff). As far as this perceptual aspect is concerned, Papa et al (2000: 93ff)

"believe that there is much to be learned by focusing exclusively on the words, stories, and accounts of women who are struggling to empower themselves in different social contexts. The difficulty of accurately representing the perceptual component of women's empowerment also guided our decision to focus only on communicative interaction. Simply stated, human interaction is necessary for empowerment to occur. Once individuals recognise their abilities to achieve desired ends, they must act in ways to reach those ends".

1.5 Nonformal legal adult education for empowerment

The role of education in facilitating access to information for individuals and groups, is of greatest importance for empowering processes. Jongepier and Appel (1995: 66) feel that

"education should be considered an important condition for attaining autonomy. Equipping people with socio-cultural, economic and political knowledge enables them to analyse their own identity and situations".

The provision of knowledge is therefore one of the decisive factors in the process (see also UNFPA 1995: 10). Since this study deals mainly with adults and adult learners, the type of information under observation is disseminated mainly through out-of-school channels, where nonformal[15] education does occur. This mode of learning should, according to Stromquist (1995: 18) be close to the person's experience and should build upon the intellectual, emotional and cultural resources of learning participants. She sees the empowerment process critically linked with the creation of physical and reflective spaces, where new ideas can be discussed and experience can be recounted amongst group members who feel they share a common problem (see also Bell 1997: 14). However, as St. Anne (1999: 69) ob-

---

[15] Nonformal education is defined as "any organised, systematic, educational activity carried on outside the framework of the formal system to provide selected types of learning to particular subgroups in the population, adults as well as children" (Coombs, Ahmed 1974: 8). In their definition, nonformal education can be distinguished from formal education (structured educational systems like school) and informal education (everyday experiences or educational aspects amongst peer groups' interaction), see Lenhart (1993: 2f). In reality, however, these categories can clearly overlap.

serves, for people to really participate, they must connect with each other in the experience they share.

Learning processes within these physical and reflective spaces are collective[16] in nature, and are mediated by a group facilitator[17]. This learner-centred approach respects experiences of all individuals participating (see also Kiiti, Nielsen 1999: 64).

Adult education for empowerment should enlighten, create an awareness and foster collective organisation. It should address strategic needs by enabling, especially, women to participate in decision-making processes within their families and communities, and to provide them with information about their legal rights (UNESCO 2002a: 19). Empowering strategies - of which legal literacy[18] is a critical tool - use methods that always include an educational component, which moves participants from learning about rights toward an understanding of the causes of their disadvantages, to the articulation of alternatives and the development of organising skills. With these skills participants are equipped to formulate effective strategies and implement action at the appropriate level in society. Power acquisition therefore happens within this dialectic between learning and organising, between theory and practice. Dialogue is a central aspect of this empowerment education (Papa et al 2000). It can be the route to mutual learning, acceptance of diversity, trust and understanding. This social learning through communicative interaction has also been associated with empowerment processes at the individual, organisational, and community levels (see Bandura 1986 below).

---

[16] According to Stromquist (1995: 18), her concept of collective learning resembles processes found in Albert Bandura's theory of social learning (see below).

[17] This facilitator, believed to be crucial to the whole process, can also be called catalyst communicator (White, Nair 1999: 48). She or he will be 'behind the scenes' to 'play the roles necessary for transformation and empowerment of the people'.

[18] The general lack of education for women leads not only to illiteracy, but also to 'legal illiteracy'. Legal illiteracy is a combination of a lack of understanding and a perception of inability to change, which can be addressed by legal literacy tools and programmes.

Information about law and various statutes and how to handle them in an individual capacity can work hand in hand with consciousness-raising and the mobilisation of target beneficiaries.

"There is the expectation that legal education will result in a positive change in familial, marital and other relationships and in the manner in which power is shared" (Agimbe et al 1994: 11).

Information can be made available to individuals, groups or the public at large. In this sense legal literacy is expected to support empowerment.

1.6 How to measure empowerment

According to Stromquist (1993), empowerment is measurable through the various components addressed by a specific programme, bringing changes in terms of individual understanding and collective action, strength and stability of the support group where learning takes place, the capacity for authority at household and community level and identifying objectives for future action (see also Stromquist 1995: 19 or Hausmann 1998: 57f). Others, such as UNICEF (in Karl 1995: 109), ALOZ (1998: 16) or Clarke (2001: 24f) support the idea of measuring five 'equality levels' of the women's empowerment framework developed by Longwe (see Hall, Mauch 2001)[19]. This framework can be used to see at which level a programme is

"to determine the point of intervention, to move women to higher levels of equality and empowerment" (Hall, Mauch 2001: 32f).

---

[19] These are the *welfare level* (this level addresses only basic needs of women; women are seen as passive beneficiaries), the *access level* (equality of access to resources as education, land and credit is needed; women notice this lack and take action), the *conscientisation level* (it needs recognition that women's problems stem from inherent structural and institutional discrimination; such beliefs are sensitised and it is pointed out that they can be altered), the *participation/mobilisation level* (mobilisation for equal decision-making alongside men in female discussion groups) and the *control level* (this is the ultimate level of equality and empowerment; women play an active role in the development process and power is balanced between women and men). The control level is, however, a pre-requisite to advance at all other levels described above.

In the view supported in this study, empowerment can be assessed through evidence of new ways of thinking, feeling and behaving, based on the individual's understanding of her or his position in society and the understanding of the type of action aimed at moulding disadvantaging social relations to her or his benefit (see also Tsanga 1998: 10).

Research suggests that the observation of a group that has participated in a programme with empowering components is needed to establish if changes are really taking place. However, this can be tricky when the output of the changed behaviour lies beyond the realm of public measurement[20]. In general, it should be noted that participatory action research could be considered a good set of tools to gain insight into at least emotional and cognitive components of empowerment, although the results can be of highly subjective nature.

In this study it will be of specific interest to see the effects of a certain communication legal educational programme on women and their families. Attitude change and a strong commitment for change with respect to all empowerment components will be indicators for an empowerment potential. This is based, first and foremost, on subjective experience of effects and changes based on the participation in a certain programme and will therefore be measured through this subjective experience of participants. The analysis in how far the outcome of the programme is favourable for the beneficiaries must be guided by what Stein calls the key to empowerment:

"However, judgements taking into account the local situation and opportunities are perhaps best made by participants. If they do not see a change in ideology as in their best interest, either the case has not been made well enough or they are correct. At the very least, if means are to accord with ends, an ideology of empowerment cannot be imposed, because the power to make decisions and to control one's own life is the key to empowerment" (Stein 1997: 63).

---

[20] To convince a person to write her or his will can be such a problem. It will be literally impossible to check how many people have really written their will and if their will is valid. This is mainly so because people tend to keep it at home at a safe place and will naturally, given the myths coring around the will in the Zimbabwean context, not discuss the existence of their will in public. Issues in health education such as condom use can be another example of this problem.

35

1.7 Bringing together women and men in the process of empowerment

Little has been reported about the productive role of men in the process of women's empowerment. Stromquist (1995: 16), for example, suggests that empowerment activities should target adult women only. While it seems that some authors assume that men are usually unwilling to participate, let alone co-operate, they do not consider that this is perhaps so because the productive roles of men are often neglected. Others simply believe that men do not want to give up power, so women should carry out their own activities aimed at taking over power. However, a closer look at the subject can reveal that these authors' basic assumption might not always be applicable to all women of this world[21].

While men exercise power over women, women do also have means and ways to exercise power over men. Women moreover do exercise power over other women - particularly in the institution called extended family.

"Power within families is perceived as being gendered yet despite the theory that women are oppressed within the family and have little real power we began to uncover through examining the lived reality of women's lives that women do have and can exercise power, particularly over other women" (Ncube et al 1997: 114).

UNFPA (1995; 2001) are amongst the few authors that stress the importance of men's participation in the process of empowerment. According to them, women can also attain autonomy at the household level when men are sensitised to get more involved in family issues (UNFPA 1995: 2; see also Hausmann 1998: 96 or Colverson 1999: 173)[22].

---

[21] It is of extreme importance to note that widely accepted concepts related to the oppression of women do not always apply to every woman. Of special importance is the denial of the general (feminist) assumption that women have been universally oppressed (Mararike 1995: 28). To say it with Papa et al (2000: 97): "Women are not a homogenous group that appear to face identical problems and share 'sisterhood' across lines of difference. The mistaken implication is that notions of gender and patriarchy are universal, context-free, and cross-cultural."

[22] Also, recent developments in the field of gender and HIV/AIDS research suggest that the focus should shift from 'man' or 'woman' to 'couple' in order to acknowledge the need for active participation of partners in this and related fields (Hall, Mauch 2001: 26).

36

Women should not be viewed as passive victims of male oppression, but as active agents constituted by and reflective of their social and cultural contexts (Papa et al 2000: 96). In having acknowledged this, women and men can be brought together in the process of empowerment (see also UNFPA 1995). Much of the information certain women should receive to challenge individuals or institutions is also new to men, and to provide them with this specific knowledge can relax situations at home (see also De Bruyn 1995: 16).

However, while discussing various issues with programme participants over the past six years, it became clear that women from all walks of life and of all ages do like to have a space where they can discuss 'female' issues amongst themselves, but feel they need to share some issues with men to achieve a progress. It is therefore crucial to consider men's roles as a part of women's empowerment. The goal of this empowerment process would then be the creation of an understanding of mutual benefit of an equal distribution of material, as well as spiritual resources and a negotiated space for both sexes, resulting in a positive change in their households and families.

1.8   Limitations

Empowerment can, as much as other concepts that deal with people and power create new problems for intended beneficiaries. As evidence suggests, an absolute non-hierarchical and participatory process of knowledge distribution is an illusion. Due to the multitude of power differences between the target group and the information source, the source will in most cases control the type of information (see also Tsanga 1998: 122).

Dependency within groups and oppression through stronger group members, the raising of unrealistic expectations (legal and social improvements do not necessarily result in equity) or the work overload for women are just a few problems which indicate that a 'radical method' discussed under 1.4 might not always be very helpful. While some authors suggest these problems are 'to some extent unavoidable' (Stein 1997: 49) and call for measures to relieve women, they do often overlook that with a different approach, these effects could have been reduced. Thus, in order to understand women's empowerment it is necessary to carefully assess the meanings women give to their specific actions and the contexts within which these meanings are situated (Papa et al 2000).

1.9 The potential of empowerment

As the preceding discussion suggests, women's empowerment manifests itself in different ways and can be explained from a number of different theoretical perspectives. The idea supported in this study is that the concept of empowerment can apply to any group of disadvantaged individuals (an 'empowerment peer group'), who are linked solely through a shared disadvantage, but this is far from making the group homogenous or a continual formation. Moreover, an individual can - through the process of learning - be in a position to address some of the issues that contribute to her or his disadvantaged situation on her or his own. However, she or he can gain more confidence about her or his action when she or he shares experiences with others. Another person or a group can assist and make her or him stronger. The goal of this empowering process is thus the self-determined, informed action of individuals and groups.

By focusing on the experiences and explanations of people, the attempt is being made to gain an understanding of how people can be empowered through communication. Empowerment is interwoven with concepts of attitude and behaviour change through communication, concepts that will be explored below.

2   Communication and persuasion

Communication, the process of sharing information and articulating social relations between people (Kincaid, Schramm 1996: 3; Siegelaub 1979: 11), can be seen in virtually every aspect of human society and it occurs at many levels[23]. The following overview of research on attitudes, beliefs, practices and ways of changing them should provide the necessary theoretical background for this study. It refers mainly to persuasive communication through film and video.

2.1 Background - the history of media effects research

Although it is known that media have effects on people, up to today there is no precise knowledge of how an effect has occurred or can occur. In his overview of research on media effects Mc Quail (1987: 251f) distinguishes between three phases:

- From 1900 to the 1930s, the common idea – based on the observation of the popularity of the media – attributed media the power to shape opinion and belief.

- From 1930 to 1960, more separate studies on effects of different types of content and media were being carried out; for example, studies on particular films and programmes. The main focus of research was on media as agents of persuasion and information. Media effects were shown to work in a pre-set structure of relationships and to operate in a particular social and cultural context. It was found that learning can occur without attitude change and attitude can change without behaviour change. As a result, the media was now believed to have a 'minimal effect'.

- From 1960 up to today, this 'minimal effect' has been strongly denied again, which is particularly due to the emergence of television in the

---

[23] According to Storey (1996: xii), there are three, such as the *individual level* of communication (it considers mainly issues like what a person says or does, what a person understands what others say or do and how a person would respond to this), the *interpersonal level* of communication (it focuses on what two or more people do or say together, affected by factors such as familiarity, length of relationship, level of knowing each other and issues of expectations and goals towards their interaction), and finally the *societal or cultural level* of communication (it refers to the "exchange and interpretation of symbols, images, and values throughout a society, usually over an extended period" (Storey 1996: xii). While communication media can affect every level, effects on one level will always have effects on other levels.

1960s and the high number of studies on its effects. To date, potential effects of media are still being sought and are, due to revised conceptions of social and media processes likely to be implicated.

2.2 Attitude formation and change through persuasion

Most of the research on media effects has focused on exploring attitudes and their characteristics. According to the findings, attitudes are reactions with a degree of favour or resentment to an object, a person, behaviour, or an event. Attitudes have an evaluative dimension (Ajzen 1993; Bohner, Waenke 2002). From this point of view, attitude can be understood as a 'multidimensional construct consisting of cognition, affect and behaviour' (Ajzen 1993: 42). It can furthermore be assumed that cognitive complexity; tolerance of ambiguity and other variables are linked to people's attitudes (Stahlberg, Frey 1996: 208-9).

Attitudes may be inherited (evidence suggests that attitudes can partially be genetically influenced. This influence might be mediated by other factors such as taste or hearing, intelligence or temperament, see Bohner, Waenke 2002: 82). However, attitudes are mainly acquired. This process happens through mere exposure (liking can increase with exposure) and conditioning. Here, learning can occur

- by contiguity: attitudes about objects can be influenced by establishing a connection between these objects and positive or negative stimuli (evaluative conditioning),

- by reinforcement: attitudes can be conditioned by reinforcement (operant conditioning) and

- by observation: attitudes can be acquired by imitating attitudes from others (see below).

Although attitudes have often proven to be poor indicators of what people actually do in real-life situations, research has supported the importance and relevance of attitude measurement to understand social behaviour.

Persuasion theories that try to explain how attitudes are formed and how they can change in response to verbal messages were mainly brought up in the third phase of research on effects from the 1960s onwards. Persuasion can be defined as

"using communicated information and argumentation from a given source to change beliefs in a target audience. Changes in beliefs, in turn, may lead to attitude and behaviour change in the interconnected attitude system" (Zimbardo, Leippe 1991: 165).

Persuasion theories can be divided into two types, namely *systematic processing* and *dual-process* models.

2.2.1 Systematic processing models

With regards to individual response and individual reaction[24] to media effects, Mc Guire's *Hierarchy of Effects Theory* (1989) suggested that the persuasive impact of a message is the product of twelve steps[25]. It is not necessary that all stages be met for a person to be persuaded, but she or he must go through many of them (Hamilton-Wray 1992: 6). This framework can explain why it is often very difficult to generate behavioural change through campaigns (Stroebe, Jonas 1996: 247).

However, although this model provides a good framework for attitude research, empirical evidence for the assumption that attitude change is determined on the reception of arguments of the message (the systematic processing of the semantic content of the message) is very limited[26].

---

[24] Defined by Mc Quail (1987: 258) as the process by which individuals change or resist, responding to messages designed to influence attitudes, knowledge or behaviour.

[25] 1) Exposure to the message, 2) attending to it, 3) liking it, 4) comprehending it, 5) learning it, 6) yielding to it, 7) memorising it, 8) retrieving it, 9) deciding on a basis of retrieval, 10) doing the behaviour, 11) being reinforced, and 12) post-consolidating the behaviour.

[26] The *Cognitive Response Model* by Greenwald (1968 in Stroebe, Jonas 1996: 247) was far more accepted, because it acknowledged the creation of different thoughts (cognitive responses) evoked in the individual through the message that are weighed against each other, whilst the individual reflects the different aspects. Attitude change is mediated by these cognitive responses, which can be favourable, unfavourable or neutral. Attitude change in the direction of the message is greatest when favourable responses outweigh unfavourable responses (see also Bohner, Waenke 2002: 131).

2.2.2 Dual-process models

This differs considerably with dual-process models, which accept systematic processing, but stress also the fact that people adopt attitudes through different factors, not only through understanding and evaluating semantic contents of persuasive messages. Eagly and Chaiken's (1993) *Heuristic-Systematic Model* focuses on what is called 'effortful systematic processing' (identical to the central route to persuasion[27]), a motivated and able judgement of the message's validity, but in absence of this, people base their decisions on non-content cues - the heuristic mode - such as characteristics of a message's source making it interesting, relevant and persuasive like credibility (is the character believable?), attractiveness (is the character appealing?), similarity (has the actress/the actor something in common with the listener?) and authority (is the character an expert to promote the behaviour wanted?).

Three broad motivational forces such as accuracy (people want to hold correct attitudes), defence (individuals want to confirm the validity of attitude positions or defend present attitudes) and impression motivation (the desire to exhibit socially acceptable attitudes, which is especially relevant when people must give their views in presence of others who are in a position to punish or reward them) are highlighted by this model and both modes of processing can serve either of the three motives (see also Stroebe, Jonas 1996: 257). The Heuristic-Systematic Model can be linked with other theories of attitude change and social influence, especially when it is admitted that people might not always be in search of valid attitudes but might simply want to defend or have an attitude that is socially acceptable.

---

[27] Petty, Cacioppo (1981, 1986) suggest in their *Elaboration Likelihood Model* two different routes of information processing such as the central route to persuasion, which leaves people spending considerable 'elaborated' time to evaluate a message (this is identical to the process suggested by the cognitive response model). If participants are unwilling to do that, there is also what is called the peripheral route to persuasion where persuasion is the cause of different mechanisms like instrumental conditioning or simple decision rules to accept a message's content.

2.3 Behaviour change through persuasion

In order to find out when attitudes can predict behaviour, Bohner, Waenke (2002: 221f) distinguish between two approaches, namely the measurement approach (how assessment measures are improved to increase prediction of behaviour from attitudes) and the moderation approach (in which personal, situational as well as content variables might moderate the strength of the behaviour-attitude relation). According to the first approach, the attitude-behaviour relation can be high when both concepts are measured at the same level (correspondence). According to the second approach, the relation can also be stronger when the attitude is strong and accessible and for people in high need of cognition, people high in self-awareness and people low in self-monitoring.

2.3.1 The Theory of Reasoned Action and the Theory of Planned Behaviour

Expectancy-value models such as the *Theory of Reasoned Action* supported by Ajzen and Fishbein (1980) and its extension, the *Theory of Planned Behaviour* (Ajzen 1993) were mainly preoccupied with establishing behavioural intentions[28] as the main determinant of behaviour. Behavioural intention is seen as a function of the following constituents:

- A person's positive or negative evaluation of behaviour performance (the attitude). This is based on beliefs about consequences of performing the behaviour,
- The subjective norm (the person's perception of social pressure as a consequence of behaviour performance). This is determined by normative beliefs (what others expect the person to do) and the person's motivation to comply.

A positive perception of a behaviour outcome, for example, will create a positive attitude towards the performance of such behaviour. A positive subjective norm then is expected when others perceive the performance of

---

[28] 'Intention' is hereby a sign of how hard people are willing to perform the behaviour (Ajzen 1993: 48).

the specific behaviour as positive. Although the two models have received a lot of support, it could be shown that habit is also an important factor (see Stahlberg, Frey 1996: 234-35). It is clear, as well, that the models do not cover all those cases, in which people are not motivated or are not capable of processing the pros and cons of specific behavioural alternatives.

2.3.2 Social Learning Theory/Social Cognitive Theory

Albert Bandura (1977) suggested that behaviour is mainly regulated through cognitive processes. A cognitive modelling mechanism (in co-operation with positive reinforcement), so he stated, can enable people to learn certain behaviour through observing it (see Wray 1991: 15). Bandura stated that people cognitively learn new behaviour through four steps, namely

1. *Attention* (it refers to observing other people's behaviour and considering their experience. This attention depends on observer capacity, past experience and situation),
2. *Retention* (the observed behaviour can only influence if it is remembered. Symbols in memory will make learning through observation possible. Mental rehearsal of what could happen to themselves helps people to remember),
3. *Reproduction* (it refers to trying the behaviour. The nature of media, particularly television and film allows the viewer to practice the behaviour through the characters, in a safe and non-threatening environment. Thus, the viewer can more readily reproduce the behaviour with confidence) and
4. *Reinforcement* (while learning a behaviour is dependent on observation, acting it or performing it follows different patterns structured by the expectation of reward or punishment. In a drama[29] the viewer's adopted behaviour is reinforced by seeing behaviour of good characters rewarded

---

[29] 'Drama' refers to a story performed by actors, recounting a chain of events and describing a web of relationships involving persons. The story follows the structure of the introduction, the development with conflict, the climax, the resolution and the conclusion (De Fossard 1996: 34).

44

and the behaviour of bad characters punished) (Storey 1996: XV; see also Hamilton-Wray 1992: 6).

By suggesting a very strong emphasis on cognition, a person's mind is seen as constructing a person's reality and performing behaviour based on expectations and values. In interaction with a person's environment and own cognition, a person's reality is being formed. To understand the processes involved in forming a person's reality will allow the prediction as well as the change of one's behaviour.

While a number of theorists have acknowledged the interaction of the person with her or his environment in learning processes, *Social Cognitive Theory* stresses activities that take place within a person; activities that influence perception as well as action[30]. According to Bandura, the following three components can be crucial in a social learning process:

a) *Efficacy*: it refers to personal empowerment and confidence in the ability to perform a certain task. This increases with experience - either self or observed, when becoming emotionally involved with the characters in a drama. Bandura defined two different concepts of efficacy, namely self-efficacy which is the belief in one's ability to organise action in order to manage different situations (1995, 2001) and collective efficacy, according to which people have the confidence in joint capabilities to fulfil set goals and to face opposition. In order to achieve change, people need to believe that they can solve their mutually-experienced problems through unified effort (see Papa et al 2000);

b) *Modelling*: role models stimulate and promote social learning and behaviour if the character is believable, attractive and similar to the viewers and if there is an emotional reaction to the model (that is if the model expresses emotion) (Bandura 1986);

---

[30] Bandura extended his model in 1978. He mainly added the factor of 'reciprocal determinism', according to which psychological functioning involves a continuous interaction between behavioural, cognitive and environmental influences. While the first three steps are identical, he claimed that once standards are set, future social inputs are evaluated in terms of situational context in which the input appears, your own internal standards as well as the possible consequences of acting or thinking in a given way. These three factors influence each other (Bandura 1986).

c) *Para-social interaction*: this concept, first used by Horton and Wohl (1956), states that individuals in the audience form relationships with characters of the media. As a result, people begin to think of fictional characters as if they were real people. Values and motives of the media character are appreciated and she or he is seen as a role model.

Social Cognitive Theory is a persuasion theory that claims behaviour can be learned through observing role models. This can occur from television or film. Film or video with a multi-plot structure can have effects on the level of societal or cultural communication in that it

"can strike a chord with its audience on a personal basis while, at the same time, reflecting the concern of society as a whole. Such drama puts people in touch with their world, helping them address their personal concerns and those of society at the same time. The most successful social change dramas are those that, because of their popularity, are discussed by many people and become a part of the society's mainstream of popular culture" (Storey 1996: XII-XIII).

2.4 The steps of behaviour change

Communication links people with one another and with their social environment. However, research shows that attitude and behavioural change rarely happens immediately upon exposure to a message. Rather, people must pass through a series of steps that lead to the desired change. While the processes and skills to reach different stages have been discussed beforehand, the actual stages are listed below. According to recent behavioural change models[31] such as the *Steps to Behaviour Change* by Cabernero-Verzosa (1996: 4), the *Stages of Change Theory* by Prochaska et al (1992) or the model of the *Steps of Behaviour Change through Communi-*

---

[31] These three models are representing similar steps or stages. While Cabernero-Verzosa lists unawareness, awareness and knowledge, motivation for change, trying the new behaviour and sustainability, Prochaska et al mention pre-contemplation, contemplation, preparation for action, action and maintenance. Piotrow et al start with knowledge and continue with approval, intention, practice and advocacy. Note that the first and the last authors assume the model to be linear, while only Prochaska et al state that the stages are components of a cyclical process, a view supported in this study.

46

cation suggested by Piotrow et al (1997: 23), five stages of behaviour change can be differentiated.

The first stage is the stage of unawareness or pre-contemplation, where an individual has a problem, but has no intention of attending to it. The second stage is the stage of awareness, contemplation or approval, where the problem is recognised (as in this specific case, through persuasion) and the person is thinking about solving it. The third is a motivation for change, a preparation for action or intention. Here, an intention to change the behaviour is present. The fourth stage is the stage of trying the new behaviour, of action or practice. The individual has enacted the behavioural change. The fifth stage, then, is the sustainability, maintenance or advocacy stage. The person has been constantly applying the new behaviour and advocates it to others. The stages are assumed to be components of a cyclical process that varies for each individual.

To be motivated to think about the message and arguments contained therein, a person must be personally involved. The person must also understand the message in order to be affected. Moreover, there is reason to believe that messages from credible (authoritative) sources will be more effective than others. Attitudes do not automatically change because a person has comprehended the message. The preceding discussion suggests that favourable cognitive responses need to be evoked, which will be best when messages relate to existing knowledge, values and interests of target groups. The quality of the message is quite important, since messages need to withstand the comparison with the already known and need to be strong to alter existing attitudes. However, this is only important if the viewers systematically analyse the message, which is the case if people are motivated and able to do so. Being distracted, for example, might lead viewers to decide on the message in a heuristic way, with cues such as credibility of the character, the attractiveness, the similarity with the viewer or the authority to see if the character is an expert to promote the new behaviour. It is extremely important that people converse about their experiences, since this can influence the thinking and motivate behavioural change (Papa et al 1995, 1997).

2.5 Facilitating and sustaining behaviour change - Diffusion Theory

Diffusion Theory suggested by Rogers (1995) mainly seeks to understand how (new) behaviour can spread through a group or a community over time. In general, information (here in particular, information transmitted through film and video) spreads best with people's similar status, experience or frequent contacts. According to this theory, groups or communities (social networks) assist people when judging new behaviour against five criteria, namely

→ Is the new behaviour compatible with beliefs and values?

→ How difficult is it to perform it?

→ Can it be tried without risk?

→ Can it be observed what happens to others first?

→ What is the advantage of the new behaviour over the old behaviour? (Storey 1996: XVI-XVII).

Film and video can communicate about issues of politics, social values, morality or religion, which then can become subjects of public debate and private discussion. The extensive discussion triggered by these programmes can shift or strengthen social or political values over time, most particularly because people expect to learn something from them. When more people discuss the programme and inform others, promoted behaviour can finally become a norm. This view integrates many different models of development communication and stresses the combined use of media and interpersonal communication (Scrampickal 1994: 14).

2.6 Persuading attitude and behaviour change through entertainment education

Entertainment education is not a theory of communication, but can be seen as a method to disseminate ideas, aimed at achieving behavioural and social change[32]. This method involves media programmes that incorporate

---

[32] The Rockefeller Foundation, Communication and Social Change Network define social change as a positive change in people's lives – as they themselves define such change (2001).

48

educational issues in the entertainment format to achieve a gain in knowledge, an attitude and behaviour change (Singhal, Rogers 2002: 118). Entertainment education programmes can be placed in the category of behaviour change communication[33].

2.6.1 Definition

Entertainment education, 'edutainment' or enter-education can be defined as the intentional placement of educational content in entertainment messages. Hamilton-Wray (1992: 4-5) defines entertainment education as follows:

> "'Edutainment' is an approach in development communication that joins together entertainment and educational elements in mass media, however an important characteristic of edutainment is that the entertainment component is dominant. In other words, the educational message is contextualised and carefully woven into the text of the edutainment piece. The five distinguishing elements of effective edutainment are that it be popular, personal, pervasive, persuasive, and profitable[34]."

The main theory behind entertainment education is Bandura's *Social Cognitive Theory* (2.3.2), which has dominated the research and the design of entertainment education ventures, mainly because it tries to influence attitudes and behaviour of the audience by making use of positive and negative role models (see Singhal, Rogers 2002: 119). The John Hopkins School of Public Health (PCS/PIP) pioneered the concept of entertainment education[35].

---

[33] Behaviour change communication is a process of understanding people's situations and influences, developing messages that respond to the concerns within those situations and using communication processes and media to persuade people to increase their knowledge and change the behaviours and practices which place them at risk (The Rockefeller Foundation, Communication and Social Change Network 2001).

[34] De Fossard (1996: 152f) extends this list by adding passionate, participatory, practical and proven effective to the list.

[35] By using entertainment to educate about health, PCS/PIP has won more than 35 international awards.

2.6.2 Entertainment education format

The format of entertainment education tools can be manifold. They can be designed for a nation, various cultural groups as well as for only a small regional group. While some producers of entertainment education tools conduct considerable research in order to design the message, others go rather by intuition. The educating section might reappear in messages or might be dealt with in a specific section. It is therefore important to consider these aspects since message reception can vary considerably according to the format and context in which it is presented (Singhal, Rogers 2002: 120).

2.6.3 Influences of entertaining education on attitude and behaviour change

Papa et al (2000: 33-34) suggest that influences stem from drawing listeners' attention to socially desirable behaviours and by developing para-social relationships with the characters in an entertainment education programme. Participants may so consider changes in their own behaviour. However, as evidence suggests media alone seldom effect individual change, but

"they can stimulate conversations among listeners, which create opportunities for social learning as people, individually and collectively, consider new patterns of thought and behaviour" (Papa et al 2000: 35).

When watching an entertainment education programme, a person must first perceive her or himself as self-efficient, before behavioural change can take place. According to Papa et al (2000: 35), para-social interaction can influence the thinking, which can lead to prompt role modelling. Then audience members can talk to one another about the message in a social learning environment, which is created. New ideas are tested, which sparks behavioural change. As far as social learning environments, or social spaces mentioned by Stromquist earlier, are concerned, the process of change can be facilitated through the communal sharing of stories on how to respond to shared experienced problems (see also Papa et al 1995, 1997 or Rimon 2002). As far as modelling is concerned, entertainment education pro-

50

grammes promote the social desirability or undesirability of certain behaviours as enacted by appealing or unappealing characters respectively. Participants can thus be provided with behavioural examples.

2.6.4 Limitations

Social and behavioural change is far from being linear, as most of the communication models suggest. When new behaviours are tested in the learning environment, external resistance from community members can occur, or beliefs may not be congruent with action (Papa et al 2000: 37). While research has found changes in knowledge, attitude and behaviour of participants of entertainment education programmes, limitations such as internal resistance effects should not remain unobserved (Singhal, Rogers 2002: 127)[36].

Moreover Papa et al (2000: 33) point out the necessity to observe social processes of attitudinal and behavioural change when studying participants' change through entertainment-education programmes:

"Entertainment-education can attract an individual's attention, which can then produce knowledge, which then leads to attitudinal and behaviour change by an audience member. This ignores, however, the complexity of social changes processes which require interaction, deliberation, and action by members of the social system".

2.6.5 The way forward

Communication theory has always concentrated on the component of persuasion; yet, the entertainment component has been mainly neglected. Entertainment education therefore provides very important insights into communication tools aimed at fostering social change. So far research has been mainly taking place in a number of developing countries and has focused mainly on radio or television. It has been found that entertainment education programmes can mould individual self-efficacy and/or collective efficacy. In attempting to change the attitude and behaviour towards women, it is sug-

---

[36] According to their observation a percentage of people from the audience identify with negative role models - an effect which must be carefully observed.

gested that these programmes have a crucial role to play. Especially when portraying women struggling with problems that the audience can understand, effects can be powerful.

3 Measuring empowering aspects of persuasive communication - a framework

As discussed under 1.6 empowering potential and empowerment processes can be measured through the various components addressed by a specific programme and the changes it brings in terms of participants' understanding of those different components that have been addressed. These changes are expressed in a changed attitude and a strong commitment for action to change. As change is measured through communication, intent to change (behavioural intention) can be used as a predictor of actual change. The following measurement components and indicators (Table 2 below) should serve as guidelines when measuring empowering potential and empowerment processes of entertainment education programmes in the course of this study.

Table 2 – Measurement guidelines

Measurement components	Measurement indicators
Cognitive components Ways of thinking	- Was knowledge gained? What type of knowledge was gained? - Were film/session messages understood and correctly interpreted? - Did this lead to an (increased) ability to name problems and to identify action leading to solutions? - Was an understanding of the need to make choices against cultural and social expectations gained?
Emotional components Ways of feeling	- Was emotion addressed? - Was a feeling of self-confidence created through the film? - Was the belief to be in a position to succeed in their efforts developed?
Political components	- Was the ability/the intention to analyse the envi-

Ways of behaving	ronment in political and social terms increased (individual awareness)? - Was the ability/the intention to organise and mobilise for social change increased (collective action)? - Is there an intention to participate in non-family groups? - Is there an intention to apply the new, promoted behaviours?
Economic components Ways of behaving	- Did messages stimulate ideas, feelings and behavioural intentions towards economic aspects of empowerment?
The attitude	Was there an agreement with the messages as a result of the interaction of different empowering components?
The behaviour Behavioural intentions	- Are behavioural intentions stated? - Are promoted messages and behaviour discussed amongst friends/family[37] or the community? Has public and private dialogue and debate expanded? - In how far are disadvantaged groups supported to voice their perspective? - What other criteria are considered to be important to assist the implementation of the new promoted behaviour?

This framework should allow insights into the different empowering components and participants' new ways of thinking, feeling and behaving, in case a change has occurred. This should be based on the target group and the individuals' understanding of their position in society and the understanding of the type of action required to mould disadvantaging social relations to their benefit.

Since this study is committed to establish the effects of a communication programme utilising audio-visual behavioural change material in the legal educational field on selected participants, effects and perceived changes

---

[37] As Rimon (2002) points out, the act of triggering partner communication is a key predictor of behaviour change, because talking to each other about the topic can be a form of information sharing or information seeking behaviour.

will be based on the subjective experience of participants as well as on their participation in this specific programme only. Effects will therefore be measured mainly through the subjective experience of participants.

Chapter II
Inheritance in Zimbabwe

1   Zimbabwe background data

The following overview of Zimbabwe's social and economic indicators in figures[38] should help to gain insight into the country's present situation before inheritance customs can be explored below.

1.1   Geography

Zimbabwe has an area of 390 580 square kilometres. Major towns are Harare, Bulawayo, Chitungwiza, Mutare, Gweru, Kwekwe, Masvingo and Marondera. Savannah and desert are prevalent and the climate is subtropical.

1.2   Population

The total population was estimated in 2002 to be 13.1 million (UNFPA 2002), with an average growth rate of 1.7 percent (as estimated for 2000-2005). The annual growth rate is suppressed by an HIV/AIDS prevalence of 25.06 percent (estimated in 1999). The age structure is 37.9 percent for 0-14 years, 58.4 percent for 15-64 years and 3.7percent for 65 years and over.

The population is divided into six ethnic groups: (*Ma) Shona* are in the majority with 76 percent and their group is further subdivided into Karanga, Zezuru, Manyika, Korekore, Rozvi and Ndau subgroups. *Matabele* (or *Ndebele)* are the second group with 19 percent; followed by *Tonga* (2 percent), *Venda* (1 percent), *Shangaan* (1 percent) and *Europeans* and *Asians* with 1 percent.

---

[38] Data for this overview has been taken from the web site of the government of the United States of America (www.state.gov/ as well as the web site of the UNDP (www.undp.org).

As far as religion is concerned, 75 percent of the population are members of Christian churches; furthermore there are a growing number of Christian sects. Animists and Muslims comprise the rest.

Languages spoken are English (official language), Shona and Ndebele as well as minority group languages.

In the health sector, the infant mortality rate was at 55 per 1000 live births estimated in 2002, while the life expectancy for men stood at 43.3 years and 42.4 years (UNFPA 2002) for women.

In Zimbabwe's formal sector, 1.3 Mio (of which 45 percent are women) are estimated to be employed. However, the informal sector is, similar to other Third World countries, extremely large.

In the field of communication, 2 per 100 people have access to newspapers, 84 per 1000 people have a radio and 27 per 1000 people have a television set.

1.3 Economy

Zimbabwe's GDP was estimated in 2002 to be at US$ 4.0 billion. However, the annual growth rate is negative (-5.5%) as estimated in 2001. The GDP per capita is estimated to be at US$ 520 in the year 2000. The average inflation rate was 230 percent in April 2003, tendency growing.

Zimbabwe has a number of natural resources. More than 40 minerals are found, amongst them gold, silver, platinum, copper, asbestos and coal. Agriculture makes up 20 percent of the GNP with main products such as maize, tobacco, wheat, cotton, sugar cane, peanuts or cattle. In the industrial sector, 11 percent of the GDP comprises of agriculture, 14 percent of industry and 75 percent of services.

The country should, given its manifold resources and good infrastructure, be self-sufficient, which it ceased to be after 1975. Sanctions, the war of liberation, structural adjustment programmes (see Kaseke 1995; 1998) as well as droughts (see Meyns 1999: 35) however have resulted in a negative growth.

1.4 Education

Education for all was a right only being granted to everyone disregarding race and sex after the country's Independence in 1980. However, up to today, access to education for girls and women is still limited, mainly due to the insufficient coverage of schools especially in the rural areas, but also due to cultural and economic constraints. Women and girls usually have much less education than their male counterparts. This gender gap is also reflected in the adult literacy rate, which was estimated in 1993 to be 89.6 percent for men and 76.8 percent for women[39]. In the nonformal field, a number of programmes aim at bridging this gap, but these programmes are carried out in certain geographical areas only and have had to cut down their operations in the last ten years.

2 Inheritance[40] in Zimbabwe

While succession law[41] systems are vast and cannot be treated here in detail, an overview of inheritance laws as well as practices in Zimbabwe

---

[39] While these figures are quite high, it is important to see the supportive environment of the years around 1995 and the manifold adult educational activities prevalent in Zimbabwe in those years. However, in 2004, this figure will certainly be much lower. This is due to a decreasing governmental investment in education with consequences such as a limited number of schools and therefore an increase in primary illiteracy. Secondary illiteracy is on the increase, too, mainly due to the lack of a literate environment supported by communication means. Moreover, if literacy levels had been measured with a functional approach in mind, the rate would have even been lower. For a definition of literacy levels, see Lenhart (1993: 48f). UNDP (2002), for example, define a literate person as anyone of the age of 15 and over who can read and write English. To which extent a person is capable of mastering the English language remains unclear with this definition.

[40] While this term is commonly used to describe the process of material property distribution (movable as well as immovable goods) to chosen people after the death of the property owner, the term *kugara nhaka*, a word which expresses the Shona idea of looking after the family of the deceased (when the deceased was male), highlights other dimensions of succession such as inheriting skills, the family name as well as people. '*Nhaka*' or '*Ilifa*' therefore includes material as well as personal aspects. *Kugara nhaka* as a process means literally 'to stay with the inheritance'.

should highlight a number of problematic issues for those who remain behind after the death of a relative and should discuss remedies implemented to counter these problems.

2.1 Traditional laws and customs of inheritance

As far as can still be recovered from oral testimonies, it is known that a marriage was traditionally registered with all extended family members being involved. In the course of extensive marriage arrangements including the payment of *roora/lobola*[42], the wife was formally integrated into her husband's family (*mukadzi wokwa*) (see also Gumbo 1998: 16). With *roora/lobola*, a family acquired the rights over sexual and other services of the bride, but did not acquire the bride herself (Weiss 1985: 41). In case of the death of the spouse a number of procedures had to be carried out before inheritance issues could be addressed[43]. When it came to choosing the ac-

---

[41] Agimbe et al (1994: 83) define law "as a set of rules used to control the behaviour of people in society. These rules regulate what people must do, what they may do and what they may not do. Law is binding".

[42] *Roora/lobola* or bride token is central to marriage arrangements, because the exchange of money or cattle will seal the relationship between two families, with duties and responsibilities. These responsibilities of the extended family should ideally include seeing to a harmonious relationship between husband and wife and any form of protection for the wife and her children. These responsibilities are valid for both extended families. *Roora/lobola* still forms an important part of marriage arrangements, although its meaning and appearance has been modified during the years. There is a big debate on whether *roora/lobola* should be abolished to support the empowerment of women (see for example Nestvogel 1985: 22-24, Heise 1989, Karisa 2003, Gokova 1997: 43 or ZWRCN 1999: 9).

[43] The following procedures are carried out upon death: After the death cry is sent out to inform the relatives, the body of the deceased is moved to her or his home area, where preparations are carried out for her or his burial. Often, a traditional healer conducts a post mortem and a cleansing ceremony to see if the person had died a natural death (*kuenda kugata/ukuya enyangeni*). The outcome of this consultation has implications on the inheritance. Potential heirs who are proven guilty forfeit their eligibility as heirs (Ruzvidzo, Tichagwa 2001: 30). After the burial, the widow has to put on a black dress, which she has to wear until one year of abstinence has passed, while a widower wears a

tual heir of the property under Shona custom, the whole group was involved. According to Ruzvidzo and Tichagwa (2001: 34), the clothes of a man were given to his brothers, (those of a woman to her sisters), the cattle to the widow and the children, kitchen utensils to the woman's sisters or their daughters; the widow and the children, the house and the husband's granary to *babamunini* (the younger brother of the husband), and the gran-

---

small black armband and can free himself from the black cloth after a short period of time. After some months, a memorial (ma*nyaradzo*) for the deceased is supposed to be carried out, where a goat is slaughtered and all family members and friends gather and sing through the whole night in order to comfort those left behind and to remember the deceased. In some areas, the clothes and personal items of the deceased are now distributed according to the wishes of the deceased or according to the rules of that particular cultural group - in most cases to the deceased's brothers or sisters. Usually one year after the death of the person, the spirit of the person needs to be brought back to her or his tribe during the *kurova guva/umbuyiso* ceremony (see also Mbiti 1974: 190). After brewing the seven days' beer, relatives gather to play the drums and sing songs of comfort for two nights. As part of the *kurova guva/umbuyiso*, which is also a cleansing ritual for the widow (she now ends her ritual abstinence and is permitted to take off her black dress), she chooses her status during the *kugara nhaka/ukungenwa* ceremony. All male family members line up and the widow is invited to choose who would be suitable to assist her and her children in the future. The widow can discuss her choice with and seek advice from her extended family members. Either she chooses to be inherited by one of the members or she chooses to remain on her own, whereby the *sara pavana* ('the one who stays with the children') would be appointed to act as a general adviser to the family (see also Weiss 1985: 42-43). When choosing not to be remarried, the widow gives the water dish (only in Shona culture) and the *tsvimbo* (traditional weapons) to her son. In any case, the widow is freed from her black dress and proves - by stepping over the *tsvimbo* without stumbling – that she has kept the mourning period and that she has not broken the abstinence rule. Then, by clapping hands, the spirit is invited into the tribe. (See Hausmann 2001: 5). Also, in some areas, the property of the deceased is now distributed as part of this ceremony, whereby a nephew or cousin displays the articles and asks all members present to whom these items should belong. It is important to note that the *kurova guva* ceremony is a central element in order to free women from being abstinent and allowing them to continue leading a normal life. "To us it is a very important ceremony because I can name more than fifty women where the relatives refused to undertake that ceremony and these families are really suffering. No jobs, bad luck" (excerpt from an interview with a traditional healer, Harare 2000).

ary and *mombe youmai (*the cow of the motherhood) of the wife to her blood relatives, the *zita* (the name of the deceased) and *tsvimbo* to the deceased's eldest son or his grandson. Ndebele custom allowed the surviving spouse (male or female) to inherit the deceased's estate (Ruzvidzo, Tichagwa 2001: 17).

As far as the position of the head of household is concerned, usually the eldest son took over, whereby he was not regarded as the universal heir but rather a family manager to replace the father when rituals needed to be carried out. In Ndebele custom, also, the eldest son took over as head of the family, but neither in Shona nor in Ndebele custom did this mean that daughters could not get a share or sons were the sole heirs. They rather managed the resources for the other family members (Stewart, Tsanga 2001: 10). However, it was clear that whoever inherited property of the deceased also inherited the responsibility to look after the widow and the children. Widows could also benefit from the chief's granary into which other members of the community had contributed in affluent years (Gumbo 1998: 16; Moemeka 1997).

As becomes clear from the above list a married woman could acquire property that could never be touched by her husband's relatives, because it belonged to her natal family only and was supposed to be returned to them upon her death[44]. If these items were not returned, the husband would have to pay at least two beasts as reparation. If these requirements were not met, the estate would not be distributed and *ngozi* (revenging spirit) would start haunting the husband's family. What also becomes clear is that Shona women could usually not inherit the house or land.

A woman's proposed lack of equality in inheritance, under traditional or Customary Law, is in most cases associated with patrilineality and patrilocal residence (Owen 1996: 53). However, there are other scholars who believe that women had actually clear property rights beyond *mawoko*. According to them, the misconception of a lack of property rights stems from

---

[44] This included kitchen utensils, *mombe youmai*, her *bonde* (bed mat), her *maphiwa* (cooking stones), her oil vessel, her waist-beads and the proceeds of her field, which are part of the so-called *mawoko* (earned with hands) (Weiss 1985: 42-43).

60

failure to further focus on the nature of traditional society. The social structure of these societies was the natural kinship family and the sole form of ownership was family. According to Dengu-Zvobgo et al (1994: 52, 87) or Siegelaub (1979), community rights to property prevailed and women had rights to property through male members of the family. Women's positions and their gender relationships were clearly influenced by marriage and kinship. As Weis Bentzon et al (1998: 106) observe, these relationships regulated behavioural patterns and affected access to resources. Such relationships could be between a daughter and her father, a mother and her son, a brother and his sister, a wife and her brother-in-law or a husband and his sister-in-law. After the death of a person, the objectives to use her/his property were clearly the maintenance and generation of the family group.

2.2   Colonial laws and customs of inheritance

While traditional laws were transmitted only verbally for generations, colonial laws were written down and distorted by male outsiders and observers. Women's inheritance rights, so it seems, started to decrease in the process.

"The minority status of women under colonial customary law has frequently been equated with women's subordinate position in pre-colonial societies. However, such a comparison cannot be made since pre-colonial society was based upon entirely different patterns of distribution and accumulation of wealth and social relations. This imposed colonial minority status has had several implications for women as regards marriage, property and inheritance as well as custody and guardianship of children" (Batezat, Mwalo 1989: 47).

Customary Law[45] or traditional laws that vary with different ethnic groups and clans, have been written down and interpreted mainly by missionaries and colonialists who have been informed mainly by men (see also Schmidt 1992). They have interpreted much of what constituted women's power as

---

[45] Customary Law has three meanings in this context: rules people cite as traditionally governing their behaviour; decisions of the tribal courts and rules and regulations accepted by European courts. Bourdillon (1975: 141) goes further to define it as "legal principles and judicial practices of a tribe modified by natural justice or morality and by certain interventions of the Parliament".

being inferior to men's, have altered Customary Law systems and have enforced them, which not only influenced the way Shona and Ndebele women were viewed, but which had severe consequences for their lives. While people defined themselves through their clan structure, the belief in ancestors and a common historical origin until the end of the 19th century, this changed drastically through laws being implemented to regulate the mobility, social lives and existence of the tribes (Schmidt 1991: 63). This process assisted in the decrease of women's status (see also Chiumbu 1997: 61). Rapid changes, access to formal education, labour migration and the accumulation of new forms of private property (such as bank accounts or houses in town), altered ethnic and local customs to the disadvantage of women (Owen 1996: 34f).

2.3 'Modern' laws and customs of inheritance

Participants of a recent survey conducted by Ruzvidzo and Tichagwa (2001: 44) state that traditional practices have indeed changed, being now a mixture of elements of traditional and Western culture, influenced by formal education, Christian religion and legal reform. Before major amendments of inheritance laws took place in 1997, the heir to a deceased man under Customary Law was his eldest male child, or his eldest female child. The heir inherited the property as 'his own subject to the customary obligation of maintaining and/or supporting his deceased father's dependants' (Donzwa et al 1995: 95). Shona practices at community level, however, also frequently appointed the eldest son as the heir. Still, the property was sometimes shared among the children and the widow and the family council dependants could appoint a widow as heir (Donzwa et al 1995: 98). Ndebele people let the family council make all decisions; here the property was shared among the children of the deceased. The widow received a share of the estate and cattle and she could use the homestead and the husband's field. Her youngest son had to stay and get married there.

Changes that have occurred in inheritance patterns led to an increase of abuse of different traditional means and rituals such as *lobola* and *kugara nhaka*. The second will be explored in detail below:

"Being an inherited wife has totally ruined my life. I cannot say I wanted to be married this way. I was forced into it. Long ago, they used to say a widow could choose to be looked after by her children, but my husband's relatives refused this. My husband had told me that upon his death I was not to be inherited by his relatives. But when he died, his relatives, especially his younger brothers took his bank passbook, saying it was their brother's money. None of my husband's relatives believed me when I told them my husband had said I should not become anyone's wife when he died but must stay and look after the children. Both my parents had died when I was just a child, so I had to be married to one of my husband's young brothers. He did not care much for me. He would come to my house once in a blue moon. And when he visited the homestead he would take away some of the furniture to sell. There was nothing I could do about it" (Getecha, Chipika 1995: 154).

Widow inheritance, a common practice in Shona and Ndebele culture, was meant to look after the widow and ensure that the children would remain with their mother in the environment of the extended family. Amongst some communities, a sexual and reproductive aspect was also crucial. Traditionally, after the death of her husband, a widow was able to choose to marry within her husband's lineage, return to her father's home or put herself under the protection of her husbands' eldest sister if she wished to remain without remarrying (May 1983: 89; Hove 1998: 12).

However, it seems that, over the years, this choice not to remarry is being refused by relatives and can, if still exercised, result in threatening or harming the widow. Relatives can take property and children and chase the woman away or they can refuse to be acquainted with the woman and reject, for example, to attend important rituals for the children. Widow inheritance is used as a means of exercising power over a woman and a means for relatives to help themselves to what they think is rightfully theirs.

"The inheritance of property, widows and children of the deceased persons by relatives is also another practice still intact but increasingly facing great resistance. In most cases, widows and children are selfishly inherited by the deceased person's relatives in order for the relatives to access the property and wealth, no matter how little is left by the deceased" (Getecha, Chipika 1995: 148).

As May (1983: 90) suggests a woman usually gives in[46] to widow inheritance without seeking authoritative advice since she fears angering the husband's family[47]. Another reason can be the fact that her in-laws would want to see her leave the home without her children, since women are believed to soon engage in external relationships, which is unwanted as long as she remains in her deceased husband's house. In order not to lose the children, some women agree to be inherited.

Closely connected to widow inheritance is the issue of property grabbing. The term stands for all acts of outsiders or family members aimed at benefiting from a deceased person's property unlawfully, thereby disadvantaging the real beneficiaries who are in most cases left destitute. Reasons for this behaviour range from traditional or cultural to sheer greed. However, property grabbing is a corruption of traditional Customary Law (Shenje 1992: 55). In cases where people cite tradition, they usually forget about the responsibilities tied to the property - looking after the widow and children (see Weiss 1990: 116).

While from 1992 onwards, many people observed that property grabbing was on the decrease, the economic hardships, faced by most Zimbabweans nowadays, have clearly caused the increase of this practice again. Inheritance has become a practical need to reduce poverty. It can occur across all ethnic, social and economic groups (Owen 1996: 60). As Chinhema (1999: 1) reports women can even be evicted from their homes after their sons have changed title deeds secretly and have then sold the house (see also UNDP 1998a: 77). While the issue of property grabbing is well known to

---

[46] A woman's reasons to consent to 'widow inheritance', however, are not always forced. How far these arrangements can also be beneficial for the woman and can support her and integrate her into the community probably depends on individual attitudes and relationships (Armstrong et al 1993: 40).

[47] A refusal to be inherited results in the loss of a woman's child-bearing capacity paid for by her in-laws, a fact that can trigger the total neglect of in-laws to see to issues of concern to her children. Some families might want to claim compensation for the paid *roora* from her blood relatives, a fact that will not help her to get any support from her blood relatives for her choice, since their first interest would be the widow inheritance and hence no compensation payments.

happen, specifically, to women (see Matope 2002: 2), more and more cases of affected widowers are being reported (Herald Reporter 2002: 2)[48]. This is especially problematic when husbands register the family home in the wife's name to safeguard her and the children, but then the wife passes away and the relatives of the wife grab the property (Chakanetsa 1992: 91). As a result, the widow or the widower and the children will remain with nothing at all, children will be expelled from school and will be forced, together with the surviving spouse, to carve out a living in difficult economic times. The rising number of children staying on the streets as well as a rising number of women forced into prostitution and into the risk of contracting HIV/AIDS proves this.

Depending on where a person resides (town, semi-urban or rural area), she or he will have options to live her or his life ignoring formal legal means but acting according to advice from community members, elders or chiefs. However, although people might enter states that are not formally considered to be valid before the law (e.g. Customary Law Unions), the consequences resulting from these unlawful states are again treated under formal law (e.g. maintenance and inheritance rights, see Donzwa et al 1995: 75f). These are reasons why each and every person needs to be informed about the laws in order to understand processes that need to be initiated after the death of a spouse and in order to prevent horror scenarios as described above.

2.4 The new Laws of Inheritance

After Zimbabwe had gained Independence twenty-four years ago, the new government implemented a number of revolutionary laws aimed at eradicating all forms of discrimination against race and sex. The Legal Age of Majority Act (LAMA) of 1982 aimed at breaking through the perpetuation of African women as minors. Business transactions, court action, bank issues as well as any form of contract, like a marriage, could not be carried

---

[48] It is now acknowledged that upon the death of the spouse, widowers also suffer from negative cultural perceptions that do not allow them to mourn openly their deceased wives (see Kapambwe 2000: 24).

out or signed by African women; instead they needed an enabling certificate signed by a brother, a father or an uncle (ZWRCN 1999: 9). LAMA enabled women to finally control their lives when reaching the age of majority with 18 years[49]. In 1991, Zimbabwe ratified the Convention on the Elimination of All Forms of Discrimination against Women (CEDAW)[50]. Then, to assist especially women married customarily (those who are most prone to abusive behaviour and are least secured through the law[51]), the extension of the right of spouses to inherit property under Customary Law have been discussed since 1992 (see Manyemba 1993: 1, 3, Gaceru 1994, Gacheru 1994, Smith 1993 or Kempley 1993: 6). This has become extremely necessary in view of a dual system of laws - customary laws next

---

[49] For a discussion on the effects of LAMA and its negative perception particularly amongst rural-based elders, see Tsanga (1998: 40f). Own research also indicates that the idea of majority is culturally unacceptable: "When one says at thirty years, you are free to do anything – according to my culture he is an infant. No one should be talking about that; you remain a child. You have your rights, ok, but not that you can say you are now free to do anything. That law is Western-oriented" (excerpt from an interview with a traditional healer, Harare 2000).

[50] CEDAW, which was adopted by the United Nations as early as 1979, states mainly following important points: "It also expressly recognises the need for a change in attitudes through education of both women and men to accept equality of rights and to overcome prejudices and practices based on stereotyped roles. Another important feature of the Convention is its explicit recognition of the goal of actual in addition to legal, equality and of the need for temporary special measures to achieve that goal. Governments should eliminate the injustices and obstacles in relation to inheritance faced by the girl child so that all children may enjoy their rights without discrimination, by, inter alia, enacting, as appropriate, and enforcing legislation that guarantees equal rights to succession and ensures equal right to inherit, regardless of the sex of the child" (OHCHR 1997:8).

[51] Customary Law Unions as well as 'kubika mapoto' (see below) are not recognised as legally valid unions. This – and the prevalence of negative social attitudes towards women - has considerable effects on the way especially female partners are treated within such unions. A study conducted in the Midlands province of Zimbabwe has clearly shown that abuse of women (psychological, sexual as well as economic) increases with the type of union. Psychological abuse is most common and highest amongst 'mapoto' and Unregistered Customary Law Unions; so is sexual and economic abuse (Musasa Project 1997: 15).

to state laws - operating in Zimbabwe. Inheritance rights depend mainly on the type of marriage a woman enters. The three different types of marriage in Zimbabwe are dealt with under different laws. If the marriage is civil, then General Law will be applied, while a registered customary marriage as well as an Unregistered Customary Law Union will be handled under Customary Law (that is, if there is no will). The different laws as well as definition difficulties have led to considerable problems in the past and much of this discussion has been incorporated into amendments of inheritance laws after 1996. A total of eight pieces of legislation are extremely important when it comes to African succession in Zimbabwe (the Laws of Inheritance in the following). They are summarised below (see also WLSA 2002; Stewart, Tsanga 2001: 11-34).

2.4.1 The Births and Deaths Registration Act (Chapter 5:02)

This act deals with the requirements of registering a birth or death in Zimbabwe. Upon registering the death of a person, inheritance processes are usually initiated. When registering, one will obtain the death certificate, without which the estate cannot be registered and no pension can be accessed. This process is the first step one has to take after the death of a relative.

2.4.2 Administration of Estates Act (Chapter 6:01)

This law deals with the requirements of reporting the estate of the deceased, the second step one has to take after the death of a relative. Here, it is important to know the marriage status of the deceased. If she or he was married according to General Law (civil marriage), her or his estate needs to be registered at the Master's Office of the High Court or can be registered at the Magistrate's Court (civil section). If she or he was married according to Customary Law, registered or unregistered, her or his case should be reported to the Magistrate's Court (customary section). It is important to note that the estate distribution under this act or its amendment (see below) will only be carried out when there is no will (in testate succession). One can say that this act lays down the procedures how to register the estate, but its actual distribution will be guided by the rules of either the Deceased Estate Succession Act (2.4.4) or the Wills Act (2.4.5). However, it must be clear that under this act, usually a male heir would be appointed and inherit in his personal capacity, which causes problems for the immediate family in case of the death of a male spouse.

2.4.3 The Administration of Estates Amendment Act (6/97)

This revolutionary amendment, which has been discussed since 1992, was implemented in 1997. The Administration of Estates Amendment Act No. 6, dealing with in testate succession, applies only to Africans who are married according to Customary Law (registered or unregistered). It allows for the first time, especially women and children, to inherit from their husband's estate, when they were married customarily. The meaning of 'heir' under Customary Law has also changed under this act: while the surviving spouse and the children will now inherit the property and are 'beneficiaries', the heir will be a person left with the name of the deceased (*zita*) and his traditional items (*tsvimbo/intonga*).

2.4.4 Deceased Estate Succession Act (Chapter 6:02)

This act lays down the guidelines of who will benefit from the deceased's estate and how. It applies to non-Africans and to Africans married according to General Law (civil marriage) only. In terms of this act, the surviving spouse is the main beneficiary. She or he and the children will automatically be entitled to the house or other domestic premises in which she or he lived before the death of the spouse and the household goods, which were used in relation to the house.

2.4.5 The Wills Act (Chapter 6:06) and the Wills Amendment Act (21/98)

The acts of succession do not apply when there is a will. The Wills Act and its amendment deal primarily with the requirements of how to write a will and when a will can be regarded as valid. In general, whoever is mentioned as a beneficiary in the will is going to benefit if the will is valid. This is the case when any person above 16 years has written and signed it, this being witnessed as shown by the signatures of two independent persons not mentioned in the will. Should major beneficiaries (such as the spouse or the children) be excluded from the will, they can seek refuge in the Deceased Person's Family's Maintenance Act (2.4.6).

2.4.6 Deceased Person's Family Maintenance Act (Chapter 6:03)

This act makes provision for the maintenance, out of a deceased person's estate, of her or his dependants. If a dependant has been left out of the will, for example, this act can help her or him to receive a share from the estate. The act will, moreover, ensure that the surviving spouse and children will continue to stay at the domicile and use all items they were using before the death of the spouse until the administration of the estate is complete.

2.4.7 The Guardianship of Minors Act (Chapter 5:08)

This act regulates the guardianship and custody of minor children. The guardian of a child born within a marriage will be the father and custody will be shared. Out of wedlock, the mother will be guardian and custodian. Issues of custody and guardianship can also be addressed in a will.

2.5 Attitudes towards the laws

There has been considerable discussion about and resistance to the new laws, mainly because they are considered to counteract tradition and customs. Ncube (1998: 171) observes that

"many of the post-independence reforming laws in the field of personal law have generated intense resentment. Often this results in the intended beneficiaries (mainly women and children) not drawing the maximum possible benefits from these laws. It is thus necessary to nurture, cultivate and develop society's receptivity to legislative reforms within the context of 'their' culture and their customs, however constructed and re-constructed".

Tsanga (1998: 94), who has discussed LAMA with rural based communities, discovered that people dismissed laws as being against the community, as being too Western[52] and as a result, as curtailing the power of elders and parents in families and communities. While some authors argue that the laws were amended radically without consulting decision-makers at grassroots level, others point out that the new laws restore what they call the real values underlying customary practices as they used to be (see for example Stewart, Tsanga 2001: 1).

When looking at the issue of writing a will, it becomes clear that myths also play a crucial role in hindering the use of state laws. While oral wills have always been common in Shona as well as in Ndebele societies, there is however a strong resentment towards writing down one's wishes. The myths dealing with written wills are endless. Here are some:

- To write a will brings bad luck; it will make you die faster,
- Beneficiaries who may want to inherit sooner can kill a person, who writes a will,
- Some men do not like to leave their property to their wives in a written will because they believe the wife will remarry, spending all his property with the new partner,
- Wills are Western and for white people only[53].

One needs to understand that oral wills are only spoken once one feels death is near. To write down one's wishes before the time seems for many people a frightening task since it requires dealing with the thought of their

---

[52] This issue comes out clearly in a discussion with a traditional healer (a male elder) on the type of information needed to restore the true values of communities in order to limit abuse in inheritance issues: "The problem is that the law is Western. The case is that we are now saying - no, the resurrection of African law and the new society and philosophy and everything else should be informed by that new ideology and the whole ideology would in most cases abrogate the colonial law and the like. It is so because the colonial laws are informed by the colonial society. We are saying that we can't have laws that are informed by colonial society since we are a society that is independent of that" (excerpt from an interview with a traditional healer, Harare 2000) (see also Zigomo 1998: 4).

[53] For further information on why wills are perceived to be for white people only and why this is historically wrong, see the article of Donzwa et al (1995: 85f).

own death. Then, people frequently feel that they lack ownership of assets worth mentioning in a will. While some think a lawyer is needed to make a will and costs to engage a lawyer are too high, others feel their illiteracy is a barrier to making a will. Then, as the survey by K2 Techtop Consult (2001) suggests, those who have decided in favour of a will do not necessarily have the knowledge to write a valid will. They will write what they think is right, and as the survey shows, that is only the case in less than 40 percent.

If one looks at the Laws of Inheritance, and especially the Wills Act, it becomes clear that most of what people fear can be avoided by taking suitable measures. There is a vital need to demystify written wills, restate the traditional value, establish role models in the community and provide information on pros and cons. After all, the oral will is very prone to abuse these days, which indeed makes it a necessity to write down one's wishes, if one wants one's family to be looked after. There is moreover a clear need to provide information on how to write a valid will in order to avoid problems concerned with the distribution of the estate or the custody of surviving children.

2.6   What hinders the use of state laws?

A number of constraints seem to hinder the use of the new laws and have led to what can be called the distinction between de jure and de facto equality (Tsanga 1998: 6). First of all, knowledge and awareness of the rights and benefits is often lacking (see ZARD 1996: 65; De Bruyn 1995: 14; K2 Techtop Consult 2001: 22f). People need knowledge about their benefits and how to pursue them. They also need to place this knowledge into their system of belief and accept it as a development that emerges from culture and from values of their respective group or community[54].

---

[54] It should not be forgotten that while not everybody is in a position to articulate one's knowledge formally, people are aware of norms and do articulate them as information acquired from different sources. In this sense, formal law, customs and practices are found among the population as 'detailed and precise discursive knowledge' or as 'applied unconsciously assimilated knowledge' (Weis Bentzon et al 1998: 184). To assume

Those who have accepted government laws and want to benefit from them also experience constraints. While new laws have been implemented, old laws have not been erased at the same time, which can result in a most unexpected and, in most cases, discriminatory solution or judgement of the matter (see also UNZCT 1998: 21). A number of inheritance disputes that have ruled against women, further discouraged many to make use of the law[55]. Apart from the lack of implementation of various acts, Gwaunza (1995: 185) lists problems hindering the benefits of, particularly, women such as their lack of finances, the general inaccessibility of courts, cumbersome and time-consuming court procedures, prevalence of men in key decision-making positions and discriminatory attitudes towards women justified on the basis of tradition and cultural practices[56]. For others, like Owen (1996: 68), it is a question of empowerment:

"How effective such law reforms are will depend on the extent to which women are empowered - psychologically, socially and economically - to go to the courts on the issues; the success of legal education campaigns; and the integrity of the local courts to administer objectively new laws on inheritance, however powerful the opposition".

---

ignorance of the law can be misleading in that people can be aware of their rights in a general sense but cannot name them in a formal legal sense.

[55] The so-called Magaya case is a good example of such an inheritance dispute between a woman and her half brother that had evicted her after the death of their father. The case became very popular, indicating that although the Laws of Inheritance were clearly on her side, it looked as if so-called traditional concepts of the family counted more in the decision made by Zimbabwe's Supreme Court (Muzondo 1999).

[56] Inheritance issues are family issues. Family issues are usually not supposed to be discussed in public. A widow, in particular, is supposed to keep quiet in order to comply with traditional attitudes concerning her behaviour as *muroora* (daughter-in-law), which state that she must respect her in-laws and even fear them (Mukunoweshuro 1992: 81). That negative attitudes are manifested at early age shows a study by Gordon (1998: 54f). She demonstrates the impact of gender stereotyping in society's perception of girl children, including their perception of themselves. Teachers and parents as well as pupils in urban and rural areas found girls to be physically, mentally, morally and emotionally weaker than boys. These stereotypes learnt at home are, as the study shows, reinforced at school.

3 Empowerment needs - communication needs

The preceding discussion of inheritance issues clearly points to the fact that problems concerning the Laws of Inheritance and their practices not only result from the conflict of traditional and modern law systems. In addition, codified Customary Law, as applied by traditional courts, presided over by chiefs and headmen, as well as the living custom, applied by different communities, interfere with each other and continue to be valid next to each other.

Apart from the simple need for information to ease one's way through the legal jungle, there are a number of urgent reasons why inheritance issues become more and more important in Zimbabwe:

- Economic hardships find more relatives engaged in irresponsible behaviour against the lawful beneficiaries of the property,

- HIV-positive widows/widowers need fast and efficient service to access benefits from their partners' estates,

- HIV/AIDS-related deaths of the heads of household in rural areas leave young women without social support and legal protection to inherit land and property, and expose them to discrimination by the community (Aggleton, Rivers 1999: 1; Government of Zimbabwe 1999, Aggleton, Parker 2002: 9). In some cases, communities and family members will refuse to allocate a widow her share of the property because they blame her for the death of her husband (UNFPA 2002: 30),

- It was assumed that in the year 2000, more than 1 million AIDS orphans were left without support and are denied the benefits from their parents' estate (UNDP 1998a: 46; UNDP 1998b). This means, at the same time, that those children will be denied their basic rights, such as schooling, since money for school fees is not available, or children are busy generating an income for survival (UNESCO 2002b: 150).

Discussing inheritance issues is part of discussing power issues. Looking at formal and informal power structures, it is suggested that women always had more say in Shona society than is formally admitted. Their power was strongest in household and extended family-related realms (so-called informal power), but a trace of female spirit mediums and headwomen shows

73

that they also had formal power. Runganga et al (2001: 317) point out that there is evidence for numerous cases where political and social decisions could not be made without women's co-operation. Women in various societies (within their gendered spaces, however) had political power and authority (Jirira 1995: 7). Thorough research on the issue

"has revealed a different image of the African woman, which indicates that she has the room to strategize within her realm to bargain and negotiate for different treatment from that which the law presumes applies or which the 'captured' images of her life indicate" (Ncube et al 1997: 11).

This is not to negate that the situation, especially for women, has been deteriorating since Zimbabwe was colonised a little more than a century ago. Additional laws implemented to regulate the mobility, social lives and existence of the tribes assisted to decrease the status of women. This had a crucial influence on the relation between the sexes.

Women from all walks of life had high hopes for an improvement of their situation particularly during the time of the Liberation Struggle[57]. Guerrillas promoted gender equality and although women fought side by side with men, evidence suggests that attitudes towards women did not really change with the new situation. Limitations of gender equality within the army and reports of incidents of male guerrillas against females clearly show that many men found it hard to accept equality in practice (see Kriger 1992: 194).

As has been shown, a number of legal means to enhance female decision-making power were implemented by the new government after Independence. However, a lack of power to make use of benefits in the legal field, mainly experienced by women, are combined with other drawbacks in society experienced on a daily basis. Disadvantages, some of them listed below, are an expression of this lack of power aimed to be addressed by the empowerment approach discussed in Chapter I.

---

[57] For a discussion on empowering effects of violent conflicts (such as the armed struggle) for women after having been exposed to social and cultural restrictions or domestic violence, see Reimann (2000: 11).

Chart 2 – Empowerment needs

Access to education:
is still limited for girls and women. Especially in times of economic hardship parents tend to again sacrifice a girl's education for the benefit of her brother. Girls are, although as grown-ups more and more accepted as an additional breadwinner in the family, still expected to get married and receive financial support from their husbands (ZWRCN 1999: 5; UNZCT 1998: 25). Higher illiteracy levels of women and girls affect issues of empowerment, particularly those in the areas of information and communication (UNDP 1998a: 76; Daily News Reporter 2003: 17).

Health information and care provision:
Malnutrition (due to poverty and cultural norms), heavy workload and poor working conditions, maternal mortality, limited contraception use (due to limited finance and control over their fertility), poor mental health, HIV/AIDS and limited access to health services (unaffordable fees in clinics, location to the nearest health facility or poor staff quality) affect the lives of all kinds of women in Zimbabwe (ZWRCN 1999: 25f; UNDP 1998a; Daily News Reporter 2003: 17; UNZCT 1998: 25).

Property and land rights:
Women remain outsiders to their husband's clan and will therefore not be granted property rights to land, which affects income control, essential tools, input and credit (ZWRCN 1999: 7).

Domestic violence:
Rape, physical assault, incest, sexual harassment, humiliation, deprivation of income and property affects women in Zimbabwe regardless of their marital status, their age, race, class or religion. Violence against women is socially accepted and tolerated by political and legal systems (ZWRCN 1999: 23; Gokova 1997: 42).

Female participation in decision-making:
Women are restricted from making decisions concerning "their bodies, minds, children, health, finances and to articulate and implement their aspirations for themselves and their communities" (ZWRCN 1999: 17).

Violations, mainly to women's rights, occur most often at the level of the family and the community. This is where legal and other systems do not reach directly. That such violations are, in most cases, the product of social attitudes, which can influence the behaviour of individuals and institutions, in public as well as private settings, makes it hard to uphold appropriate policies and regulations for rights protection.

The inheritance issue and all other issues mentioned in Chart 2 above are interconnected and deal with negative attitudes resulting in negative behaviour that brings disadvantages for those who lack power to act accordingly.

Awareness of the negative consequences of these attitudes, especially in the inheritance field, seems to be present amongst many communities in Zimbabwe. As recent research suggests, there is an awareness that inheritance brings along family conflicts, disagreements and violence. Greed, the cruel treatment of orphans, the disregard of moral norms, the neglect of matrimonial property, problems caused by polygyny, property grabbing and fear of avenging spirits are issues of importance to various communities in Zimbabwe (RSC Zimbabwe 2001).

However, there is a clear need to increase a rights awareness of individuals and groups. Myths and misconceptions about legal as well as other issues reveal the necessity for communication and dialogue about those conflict areas. How this should be achieved using film and video will be discussed in detail in the next chapter.

Chapter III
The use of locally produced message films in nonformal adult education in Zimbabwe

1 Media and communication in the African context - film and video in Zimbabwe

An overview of media and communication in the African, and in particular, in the Zimbabwean context will highlight why film in particular can be a suitable medium for change. Reasons are explored below.

1.1 Why film?

Communities and groups in most of the countries of this world have always had means and ways of ensuring intra- and inter-group communication. As a means of sending messages in a given community, community media could be verbal (songs, drama, proverbs), non-verbal (gestures, facial expressions) or symbolic (rituals, artefacts, tokens). Ethnic groups in Zimbabwe have, up to today, a performance tradition; their traditional folk media aim at transmitting messages and information through songs, dances, drama, mime, puppets, story telling, oral poetry and proverbs (FAO 1998: 8).

Film and video as tools to disseminate information can have a marked influence on society not only by transmitting information and knowledge or by entertaining, but also, by mobilising people and persuading them to adopt new behaviour (Scrampickal 1994: 13, Mc Quail 1987, Aufderheide 2002). In the villages, due to oral tradition impacts, people normally think in images and visuals. Film and video can translate thoughts and abstract concepts into identifiable experiences to be shared (Scrampickal 1994: 20). As an educational tool, film can deepen the power of comprehension and memory.

"A person typically retains about 10 percent of the information (s)he reads, 20 percent of what (s)he hears, but a full 80 percent of what (s)he sees and hears and discusses. This is the potential of an audio-visual projection as a teaching tool" (FAO 1990: 5).

Used in adult education for empowerment, it could make people act, adopt new practices and form new habits because of messages that show them how they can benefit.

1.2 Characteristics of film and video as educational tools

When looking at the different characteristics attributed to film and video by various agents of change, it transpires that the use of film and video in adult education is perceived to bear a number of advantages as well as disadvantages. Advantages named by FAO (1990: 4), for example, are that video usually reaches a wider audience at one time and transcends, at the same time, the problems of illiteracy. Audio-visuals, therefore, allow people to absorb more information. Film, so others state, uses both sight and sound and can therefore attract attention and make great emotional appeal to large audiences. It compresses time and constricts space differences and is therefore a highly persuasive and effective communication medium (FAO 1998: 13). Especially the impact of images is perceived to be great, since they are a criterion of the credibility of the message (Schwarzkopf 1989: 45). Maruma (1993: 52-53) feels that film has made instruction so individualised that it can be used to meet the specific needs of the underprivileged as well as over-privileged. It can assist in areas where trained teachers are lacking and thus help to equalise learning opportunities.

Disadvantages listed are, for example, that video is a less intellectually stimulating means of communication (FAO 1990: 4), especially when there is a lack of personal contact between the emissions and the recipients (Baacke 1994: 455; 1995). Others feel that film supports a continued dependence on foreign imports and foreign experts and that it provides one-way communication unless used in smaller groups. Moreover, film in a vacuum is perceived unlikely to have a long lasting effect (Wray 1991: 28). Numerous communication studies have revealed that communication through film and video encourages attitude change[58]. Films can present models, confer status and suggest appropriate behaviour. However, film and video use is perceived to be most effective when messages are discussed in groups. An important aspect of this discussion is to obtain the audience's opinion about the film or the video and the subjects covered.

1.3   Film in Zimbabwe - the background

In Zimbabwe, film and its production as well as its distribution has always been a task of the Ministry of Information. Before Independence, the Rhodesia Production Services was mainly occupied with the production of educational films (agricultural instruction and the like) and propaganda films to find more supporters of Liberation War efforts in especially rural areas. Films were mainly brought to their target groups through the Mobile Film Units of the Rural Information Services, which had as many as thirty vehicles travelling through the country, thereby reaching a third of the rural target groups (Riber 2001: 1). Mobile Film Units were mainly sponsored through advertisements from the private sector.

However, since Independence, the impact of the government-owned Mobile Film Units, as well as Production Services, has been limited mainly due to the harsh economic climate. Private companies and NGOs have taken over film and video distribution and production.

1.4   The production of African films

For a long time, mainly foreign productions were screened in Africa, which did not allow viewers to really identify with the characters. That is one of the reasons why for most of today's Zimbabwean filmmakers, film is seen as a medium of communication, a medium they employ with passion

---

[58] The use of film/media can go beyond the mere screening and discussion of existing films. The concept of 'Development support communication', which has been utilised since the mid 1960s, can be most powerful by involving people in the making and discussion of programmes and films. It can help to awaken people's critical awareness and their readiness to express needs and opinions (see Ramirez 1999: 87).

(Monaco 1981: 278). However, as far as film production is concerned, there are only a handful of companies and NGOs active in Zimbabwe to date[59]. The biggest is Media for Development Trust (MFD), which has produced as many as nine feature films and a number of short films so far[60]. MFD, a local non-profit social welfare organisation, seeks to provide development through communication in Zimbabwe, and Africa as a whole, particularly through the production and distribution of high quality, socially conscious films and videos.

1.5 The distribution of films - media use in Zimbabwe

Film distribution happens via four channels, namely cinema, television, video and private mobile film units (road show advertising). While cinema used to be one of the most frequented channels - Riber (2001: 3) states that Zimbabweans are very active film goers and once formed the second largest market in Sub-Sahara Africa - economic hardships and specifically the lack of foreign currency led to closing down most of the cinemas, leaving Zimbabwe with approximately 30 cinemas throughout the country.

The only television network in Zimbabwe is owned and controlled by the government. If new films are produced, the unavailability of television sets for most will make it hard to benefit from them[61]. An alternative to state television is satellite television as well as a number of video libraries.

The last channel is the use of private mobile film units, or road show advertising. Mobile film units that are mainly utilised by private companies and NGO's advertise a client's product in ways that can reach rural as well as urban audiences. By using mainly traditional teaching and entertainment

---

[59] Zimbabwe has no real film industry, mainly due to constraints such as marketing problems, no co-operation of scriptwriters on joint ventures and lack of adequate funds to develop a sustainable film industry (Karikoga 1999, see also Pfeiffer 1993: 62).

[60] These are, amongst others, the well-known films 'Consequences' (1987), 'Jit' (1990), 'Neria' (1992), 'More Time' (1993), or 'Yellow Card' (2001).

[61] A recent study on media access by rural households in Buhera District confirms that television sets are hardly available and will, if used to disseminate educational and developmental information, exclude the majority of households (Matewa 2002).

strategies, such as drama, question and answer sessions, quiz shows with prizes as well as film and video, road shows provide often the only entertainment source for the region and therefore usually draw large crowds. Road show vehicles tour the country according to pre-set routes for six months up to one year. At present, two road show companies are active in the field. One road show company with only two vehicles is able to reach around 2.5 million (mainly disadvantaged) people in a year.

1.6 Film and video for social change in Zimbabwe

In Zimbabwe, the concept of entertainment education for social change has, mainly, been applied by MFD. According to MFD's director John Riber (1993: 19), a powerful entertainment education tool needs a dramatic story, the involvement of local people in all aspects and the messages to be wrapped in a good story. This includes issues such as the familiarity of culture as expressed through language, the environment and the behaviour of characters in the films. The latter especially seems to be one of the strongest inputs for a film to be credible (Ghosh 1984: 64). To include all these issues when making a film, participatory action research and a general participatory manner in planning, design and implementation phases should be employed.

In order to heighten identification possibilities for, especially, rural audiences, Riber (1993: 19) suggests the dubbing of the production into local languages and the use of television, mobile film units and video renting libraries as distribution channels. Only then can film and video have potential for empowerment and social change for its audiences.

2 'Neria' - a Zimbabwean entertainment educational tool

Conversation 1:

PHINEAS: "Come off it man. Look, there's a fishy story there. You know, the last time we were together he told us he had just written a will. Next thing we know he's dead.

FRIEND 1: He probably knew that he didn't have long to live, so he wrote a will. What's wrong with that?

PHINEAS:	You don't understand? He must have told his wife that he had just written a will!
PATRICK:	What would she kill him for?
PHINEAS:	For the money, of course... the money.
PATRICK:	But he earns money to take care of the family. If he is dead there will be no more money coming...
PHINEAS:	Patrick, I'm beginning to get worried about you. You put too much faith in these women. I suppose when you and Neria got married you wrote a will, eh?
PATRICK:	No, we don't have a will. But it's a good idea..." (Riber 1992: 21-22).

Conversation 2:

CONNIE:	"There is something you can do besides borrowing money.
NERIA:	What? Except wait and hope.
CONNIE:	I know a man... a lawyer, who helped me during my divorce. Why don't you see him?
NERIA:	How can the law help? There was no will.
CONNIE:	Never mind the will. Even without a will you can get what belongs to you.
NERIA:	But it must be very expensive. I can't afford it!
CONNIE:	I could lend you the money until your case is sorted. Or you could go to the legal NGOs for free legal advice.
NERIA:	How can I fight my children's own blood?
CONNIE:	Don't worry. I was afraid at first. But I learned I had to understand the laws and use them to protect myself.
NERIA:	I don't know... I need to think about it" (Riber 1992: 47-48).

These two conversations appear in scenes of *Neria*, Zimbabwe's most popular feature film on inheritance-related problems, produced by MFD in 1992. They could have happened (and are probably happening) in any corner of this and other Southern African countries, because they reflect common myths, fears and concerns of everyday people confronted with death, the law and the specific cultural implications surrounding death.

2.1 Background

Neria is a production from the production house, Development through Self-Reliance Inc. (DSR), in the United States and its non-profit branch, Media for Development Trust (MFD), in Zimbabwe. This production house has pioneered the field of entertainment education in Africa by producing and distributing social message films and videos that entertain people while educating them. A thorough research, design and production phase usually makes films from MFD very special. Moreover, these films have a high quality as international awards suggest (Hudock 1993: 7).

Neria was the second feature film in Zimbabwe initiated by a Zimbabwean filmmaker and was realised with an overall local crew in 1992[62].

---

[62] The idea for a women's film project dealing with problems for women concerning inheritance issues was brought to MFD in 1989 by Godwin Mawuru, who himself had experienced conflicts with demanding in-laws, when his father died. For nearly two years, MFD developed the script, undertaking thorough research in order to directly learn from the audiences about their needs. In particular, an advisory panel of 12 local experts on law, women's status, culture, anthropology and writing, was formed for six months, looking at the complicated issue of African women's being affected by inheritance rights between traditional customs, Southern Rhodesia's colonial laws and independent Zimbabwe's modern laws. Moreover, focus group discussions and key informant interviews in different regions of Zimbabwe were carried out to identify main messages the film should carry. On the basis of these findings, Tsitsi Dangarembga, a famous local novelist, who is well known for writing stories about Zimbabwean women caught between tradition and modernity, was asked to write the story. Louise Riber from MFD then converted this short story into a screenplay. With the assistance of international donor agencies (CIDA, Sida and NORAD), the filming began in October 1990 with an overall local crew and Godwin Mawuru as the film's director. After the film had been completed, it was pre-tested in Zimbabwe, Botswana, Kenya and Ghana. *Neria* finally started running on March 20 1992 in Kine 400 in Harare and stayed in the cinema for the next six months, breaking all box office records and outgrossing even famous American productions (e.g. Terminator II) (Hausmann 1999: 6-7). Apart from being the most successful local film ever shown in Zimbabwe, *Neria* gained international attention as well as the following awards suggest: MNET award, South Africa (3rd best film; best actress; best musical score), OAU award Carthage Film Festival, Tunisia (best director), Black Filmmakers Hall of Fame, Inc., USA (best foreign film), 8th Black International Cinema, Indiana University, Berlin (best film by a Black filmmaker), Prize from the Public; OCIC Prize, Milano (in Hudock 1993: 7).

2.2 Neria - the story

The 'modern' couple Neria, a seamstress, and Patrick, a carpenter, lead a harmonious and equal relationship and are residing in one of Harare's high-density suburbs. They have two children, Mavis, a daughter, and Shingayi, a son. Neria works at a crocheting co-operative. Some months, she manages to earn more than her husband.

Patrick and Neria have been living in the city since their marriage, but they keep up the relationship with their rural-based in-laws, portrayed by Patrick's mother, Ambuya, Patrick's elder brother, Phineas, and his wife Maria. As antagonists, they represent the opposite of Patrick's nuclear family. Ambuya is always trying to convince Patrick to leave Neria, who, she thinks, is too modern and does not know a woman's traditional tasks. Ambuya does not understand the modern lifestyle and thinks Neria should stay at home. Neria respects these ideas and tries her best to please her mother-in-law.

Phineas, who is a dominant personality, also tries to change Patrick's mind about Neria, mainly because he cannot understand why Patrick discusses every issue with Neria. For Phineas, women are supposed to be submissive to men, and Phineas treats his wife Maria accordingly. Maria sees no other option but to stay with Phineas in order to be looked after.

There comes the day where Patrick does not return from work. He dies on his way home after being run over by a car. Neria is devastated. She and the children go to Patrick's rural home for the funeral. However, after a month, Neria feels she must go back to the city - they must continue their life. In the meantime, Phineas has helped himself to all of Neria and Patrick's property, which he has transported to the rural areas. Neria and the children are left with nothing and are struggling to make ends meet. Phineas is abusing his traditional role as the protector of his late brother's family and refuses to assist them.

Neria's friend and neighbour, Connie, a divorcee, and the other women of the co-operative are the only ones who provide moral support. Connie advises Neria to go to a lawyer, but Neria is reluctant, as she feels this would be an offence to her husband's relatives (see conversation 2 above).

After some time, Phineas and Maria decide to stay at Patrick and Neria's house in town and they try to win over the children. Neria's suffering continues. When she returns from work one day, the locks at her house have been changed and the children are gone. Phineas has taken them to the rural areas without permission, so Neria goes after them. When she arrives at the homestead, she finds her daughter Mavis very ill and under no care. Phineas once more refuses to assist. Neria carries her daughter on her back to the bus stop, and to the hospital where she can have an operation just in time. Neria is now convinced that she must take legal action. When she finally visits the lawyer Mr. Machacha, he explains all the necessary steps she must take in order to register her husband's estate. With the help of her brother Jethro, Neria goes through the necessary legal channels and her daughter is appointed heir of the property. Phineas is ordered to return the property.

However, Phineas does not give up. He feels he is entitled to his brother's property and takes the matter to the High Court, claiming that Neria is not fit to maintain the children. After a court hearing, Phineas' exploits are brought to light and the judgement is in Neria's favour.

The final scene is the traditional *kugara nhaka* scene in the rural area one year after Patrick's death. Neria decides not to remarry by giving the traditional items to her son, Shingayi. Ambuya has, through the unlawful actions performed by Phineas, come to the understanding that Neria was supposed to take care of children and property right from the start. She sees that genuine tradition would have wanted Neria to be looked after and she condemns Phineas' behaviour as greedy. Ambuya realises that Phineas has twisted tradition to suit himself. She comes to understand that sometimes tradition must bend with the changing times. In the last scene Neria and Ambuya shake hands in understanding.

2.3 Film goals and messages

As a so-called women's education project, the film showed for the first time disadvantages a woman in Zimbabwe could face upon the death of her husband. It should cover basically the following fields:

"- Provide basic information (in layman's terms) about the current legal status of women and encourage widowed women to use legal means, within their social context, to resist exploitation (differences between Customary and Common Law, importance of wills, birth and death registrations, basic knowledge about key acts such as the Legal Age of Majority Act (LAMA) and the Deceased Person's Maintenance Act),

- Present traditional merits for widows within Customary Law (Customary Law has played and always will play a very important role in traditional society. Conflicts between Customary and Common Law often result because of differences in lifestyles. Women must be prepared for the social consequences of moving away from traditional customs),

- Encourage women to be self-reliant (to develop income generating skills allowing them to become financially independent if widowed),

- Encourage policy makers to provide more protection for widows,

- Promote the importance of planning for the security of women and children in the event of the husband's dying (communication between the immediate and extended family regarding these matters and the devastating effect of the widow issue on children),

- Present common ways in which widows are taken advantage of (by insisting that they are inherited into the family even against their will; through holding property, money and children at ransom until the widow agrees to inheritance; by taking advantage of them when they are under the stress of mourning their husband's death; through accusing them of killing their husbands if they do not agree to inheritance and through encouraging their children to turn against them when refusing inheritance)" (Matsikidze, Mawuru 1989: 7).

Neria should encourage awareness among women and men about the issue of women's rights yet maintain a primary emphasis on being entertaining. The film should serve as a positive example to encourage women, men and communities to examine their own positions regarding women's rights.

Educational goals core around themes such as traditional inheritance versus modern laws of inheritance, the breaking up of family structures and the change of values, gender equality and traditional gender roles, domestic violence, children under stress, socialisation aspects, or women's empowerment.

2.4 Reasons for the success of *Neria* - the preliminary study

Neria has reached, through a variety of distribution channels, a widespread audience in different parts of the world. Why it was especially well received in Zimbabwe was one of the questions the preliminary study (see 0.2.1) tried to answer. It was found that the overall response towards the film and its messages was highly positive, making *Neria* a success not only in terms of high audience numbers, but in terms of messages being received and actions being taken. The film helped women to be aware of their problems and offered solutions to them, led men to new insights and promoted the necessity of writing a will. It, moreover, promoted the necessity of legal changes in favour of widows, which led to the Administration of Estates Amendment Act by the Government of Zimbabwe (see Chapter II; 2.4.3). It was found that since the laws had now changed, the film needed revision (Hausmann 1999; see also Stewart, Tsanga 2001: 2). A further distribution of the film could be highly recommended, although it was suggested that a short version of the film (a support video) should be created, accompanied by a support manual. Some of the results of the study are highlighted below.

2.4.1 The use of *Neria* - NGOs and other stakeholders

Apart from cinema and television screening, NGOs in Zimbabwe and other African countries can be regarded as the main promoters and users of the film. As far as the African continent is concerned, they play the most vital role in facilitating grassroots distribution of 16 mm/35 mm films as well as videos, thereby allowing a large number of their members to have access to educational and entertaining films. *Neria* has been used to entertain and to educate a variety of different target groups. Mainly local organisations and institutions have used it for the training of resource persons like trainers or staff from other organisations. Where the film was shown to members of their groups, it was incorporated into workshops on a variety of topics such as gender sensitisation, family planning, HIV/AIDS awareness, awareness on domestic violence, civic rights or inheritance rights awareness.

When *Neria* was released, main legal rights NGOs utilised the film as a lobbying tool within their inheritance awareness campaigns, mainly to respond to the White Paper on Marriage and Inheritance from 1992/3, where the issue of spouses and property had just become relevant.

"WILDAF together with a number of organisations worked around the screening of the film Neria in 1992. Members went to local cinemas to circulate some information flyers to audiences both before and after the screenings. This was aimed at letting members of the public know how they – like Neria – could fight for their rights if they ever had a similar problem" (WILDAF 1993: 1).

It was reported that, after the film was shown in the cinema, it was a lot easier to target problems concerning inheritance. People could talk about legal issues, referring to 'the problem Neria had'.

"Like Neria, the heroine in the locally made feature film of the same name, and like thousands of other women in Zimbabwe… (she) was not aware that the law could protect her from greedy relatives' intent of taking advantage of her situation, citing tradition and custom. Without a will, however, a woman can find herself, as Neria did, in a situation where she has to fight in order to get any share at all" (Enochs 1992: 37).

These discussions resulted finally in the amendment of the Administration of Estates Act (November 1, 1997); now ensuring, especially widows with unregistered marriages, more rights in keeping their estate (see point 2.4.3 in Chapter II). Although it is hard to prove how far *Neria* actually convinced the government to change the legal situation for widows, lawyers and legal rights NGO personnel all shared the strong belief that the film and an increased legal awareness of women were the main factors for the change:

"*Neria* provoked enormous discussions, most of the legal rights groups were using the film within their awareness campaigns. It definitely sent messages to the authorities. The 'Inheritance Act' was then already in discussion. *Neria* really is a good example of how laws are invoked in people. Usually a new Act is released and then awareness campaigns start. In this case it was just the other way around. A dialogue on what people really wanted to see in the Act was created first which then led to the release of the Act. Some episodes in *Neria* really sent shock waves to the people. What you could see in the film was exactly what was happening out there. It certainly is a great tool for awareness raising and without the film it would not have been possible to create an awareness like that amongst politicians, organisations and individuals" (excerpt from an interview with a female judge in Hausmann 1999: 20).

2.4.2 Popularity of the film

"This film is about awakenings - the audience's awakening to a different culture, Neria's awakening to social empowerment and, hopefully, Zimbabwe's awakening to a new day" (Weathersbee 1993: 26).

Judging from film reviews by a variety of national and international newspapers and magazines, on the one hand, and answers from interview participants on the other, there are a variety of reasons, why *Neria* was so well received and still is such a popular film.

"The optimistic message the film puts forth is twofold: that an African woman can fight back through the courts and win, and that tradition can be adapted to fit a changing world. It is an encouraging and uplifting proposal, one that has obviously found a receptive audience among both women and men who identify with the victim of this insidious problem rather than with the villainous brother-in-law who perpetrates it" (Hill 1993: 66).

Apparently, the film was released at a very pertinent moment. Independent Zimbabwe's new laws had been implemented for just a short while, which created the need to supply information especially on inheritance issues. Since it was (and still is) rather taboo to talk about problems that occur in a family, it was probably a catalyst for most of the people watching it. Seeing it actually happen and seeing the reactions from the audience might in most cases have facilitated a possibility for frank discussion, which presumably had a relief effect. At the same time, it respected African attitudes about taboo issues involved like sex or violence.

After a long period of limited access to films during the colonial period, *Neria* dealt with issues the average Zimbabwean could identify with.

"Neria packed them in at commercial movie houses after its release on March 20, 1992. The film stayed in the theatres for six months, outgrossing even Terminator II and it reached the rural population that normally does not go to the movies. People made pilgrimages to the cities, where it played or organised car pools for the drive-in shows" (Hill 1993: 65).

Written and directed by Africans, dealing with a burning issue in Africa and showing African surroundings, *Neria* is a film created for African audiences. Issues that are dealt with in the film are so common that a variety of different viewers can all identify with some parts of the film somehow.

"A widow stripped of her inheritance rights, her villainous and demanding in-laws and biased traditions are the rudiments upon which Neria was made, projecting an almost perfect portrayal of a realistic Zimbabwe, which African audiences can identify with" (Chikambi 1992: 6).

Another aspect, which increases the film's popularity, is the combination of musical interludes, folk tales, legal instruction and traditional narrative, a mixture that people perceive as 'truly African'.

Many mentioned the acting as well; according to them, the actors managed to play their roles in an excellent and convincing way.

"I think the reason why everyone liked the film was because of the way they were acting, especially Neria. Every African woman would know that it is just like that, that in reality it is not just a film but shows our experience. Yes, they were acting, but you know, it was real" (excerpt from a focus group discussion with female dressmakers and vendors in Hausmann 1999: 19).

Addressing cultural constraints and showing them in an exaggerated way, the typical behaviour of everyday people allowed high identification possibilities for the audience.

2.4.3 Impact of the film

As an effect of having watched the film *Neria*, it was reported that more women sought advice from legal NGOs.

"Many women actually came to seek advice after having seen the film and many of them realised that it is better to have a registered marriage" (excerpt from an interview with a female programme co-ordinator in Hausmann 1999: 20).

They brought their cases to court.

"You know, when I went to court, I saw that I was not alone, all those women were there, they had similar cases" (excerpt from an interview with a widow in Hausmann 1999: 22).

As a lawyer from a legal NGO suggested,

"As far as the court was concerned, people were definitely more aware that they could at least bring in a case like that. Women were definitely empowered by seeing that Neria made it happen and succeeded" (excerpt from an interview with a female judge in Hausmann 1999: 22).

2.4.4 Feedback on *Neria*

One positive aspect mentioned frequently by resource persons was the fact that the film immediately created prolonged discussions about the behaviour of the main actors and cultural issues in general.

"The film generates debate, it helps to put down barriers. While a woman in the homestead will not necessarily be able to address issues like that, she is able to do so after she has seen the film with her husband. It really opens up people; they start talking about their culture. With men, especially the strong traditionalists, we experience a breakthrough. When we show the film to chiefs or village heads, who were beforehand not willing to discuss gender or AIDS issues, they really open up and want to discuss" (excerpt from an interview with a male project co-ordinator in Hausmann 1999: 23).

The information provision, the explanation of legal contents in a clear way in the film was mentioned to be a very positive factor as well. It was reported, that

"all participants are instantly requesting more legal information after having seen the film, information on the legal system, on how they can proceed with their individual case and which resources they can draw back onto" (excerpt from an interview with a female programme co-ordinator in Hausmann 1999: 24).

As a widow testified after having seen *Neria*:

"I watched it on TV because people were talking about *Neria* all the time, they said I had to see it since the same thing happened to me. When I watched it, really, it was very interesting for me because it was exactly what my brother-in-law did to me. A week after my husband died my brother-in-law was asking for my bankbook, every member of the family wanted something from me. I had a registered marriage without will, just like Neria. After I came back from a visit from the rural areas, my in-laws had taken my things. They were threatening me so much and harassing me, although I was still mourning, I never had time to rest. (…) You know, with our African custom, people want to leave you with nothing at all. Until now, I am suffering the consequences, although most things went well. When I saw *Neria*, it was like me, it was exactly the same" (excerpt from an interview with a widow in Hausmann 1998: 24).

2.4.5 The need for continuity

Asked if and in how far people still wanted to use *Neria*, a clear positive reaction could be recorded. This was mainly due to the fact that the situation for women has - though improved due to the Laws of Inheritance - not really changed at community level. Inheritance-related constraints have, so it was recorded, not lost their topicality:

"Neria's problem is still a burning issue. Even in the towns the so-called educated are not fully aware of the contents of the law. In general, the knowledge what to do and where to turn to for assistance in case of rights' violation is lacking. Many women still do not know what to do. If they know, they are in most cases hindered to take up action by the usual constraints such as no money or nowhere to stay in town. They give up or give in into widow inheritance. At the same time, even if awareness is raised, the services are simply not there. It needs certain groups to interact and sensitise, because you probably manage to empower women through the film as the film is real for many and everything went well for Neria, but what happens if things are not going too well for the woman in court? What, if she cannot even make it there because she is left with no money at all? Women will be even more disappointed. That is why obstacles have to be discussed in order to fully empower women. The service providers also have to be sensitised. And all that is in vain if the environment of the woman is not supportive" (excerpt from an interview with a female research officer in Hausmann 1999: 32).

2.4.6 The way forward

Despite the positive outcome the film has had so far, there is still a great need to use the film in the future. Apparently, many regions of Zimbabwe have not been covered and there is - according to reports - still a lack of knowledge and awareness on the side of women and men. Given the external constraints, like poor infrastructure in the rural areas, or a slow willingness to change (sometimes distorted) customs and tradition, the film needs to be distributed continuously for years to come in order to reach the people for whom the film was made.

How *Neria* was further developed and distributed after the preliminary study will be shown in the following chapter.

Chapter IV
Participative strategies for the design and distribution of training material for *Neria*

1 The *Neria* Grassroots Distribution Project

Although many people have watched *Neria,* the need to disseminate inheritance-related information and to create an awareness that can lead to positive attitudes and likely, also, to behavioural change remained great, due to the reasons discussed in Chapter II and III. In the following, a project aimed at bridging this gap, the *Neria* Grassroots Distribution Project, implemented during 2000 and 2001, will be described in detail.

1.1 Background

This project was based on data and experiences gathered in the preliminary study of the feature film *Neria* in 1999 (as described in the preceding chapter). As the research suggested, the full potential of the film had not yet been realised. One of the findings of the research was that due to the instructional nature of the *Neria* feature film, it was being used more and more within various education and training programmes of NGOs, recently also at grassroots level, but it lacked proper training material suitable for the variety of target groups wanting to benefit. Moreover, in the face of legal changes in favour of widows in Zimbabwe, it seemed crucial to update legal information provided in the film, to dub the feature film *Neria* into Zimbabwe's major local languages, Shona and Ndebele, to develop educational supporting material such as a support video and a support manual for the film, and to distribute this material through chosen groups to the grassroots all over Zimbabwe.

1.2 Objectives and main beneficiaries

The objectives of the project were to

- place the film *Neria* in the context of learning and training to enhance the empowerment of its target groups,
- heighten identification possibilities for target groups and their communities through vernacular versions of the film and supporting material in order to raise awareness so that steps could be taken for action on behalf of women's issues in general and inheritance-related problems in particular and to
- develop/support networks for the use of video in gender sensitive education and training programmes at community/grassroots level.

The project was aimed at benefiting disadvantaged people in rural, peri-urban and urban areas of Zimbabwe, who have not yet had the chance to see the film. Moreover, the material should suit mainly non-professionals, working with communities in rural, peri-urban and urban areas of Zimbabwe.

2   Project phases

The following three main project phases of the *Neria* Grassroots Distribution Project were carried out:

Phase 1 - The dubbing of the feature film *Neria* into Shona and Ndebele,

Phase 2 - The development of educational support materials including a support video focusing on the key learning points of the feature film and a support manual to facilitate learning with target groups,

Phase 3 - The implementation of a grassroots distribution campaign to reach disadvantaged groups across Zimbabwe.

They are described below.

2.1   The dubbing of *Neria* into Shona and Ndebele

The film script was revised after extensive consultations with lawyers and was translated into vernacular Shona and Ndebele. The film was then dubbed and edited. A pre-test copy of the English, Shona and Ndebele support video was designed. Having conducted all the necessary research (see below), voice-over narration was recorded and final editing carried out. Video masters for VHS video copying were created and printed.

2.2 The development of educational supporting material

Following mainly the Hopkins P model developed by the John Hopkins University Centre for Communication Programmes (JHU/CP), the development of support materials was done in five main steps and a number of sub-steps to suit the various communities' needs[63] (see Table 3 below).

Table 3 – Data gathering steps of the Hopkins P model

The P model	Steps taken for this study
1. Analysis	– Data review, preliminary study, preparation and planning
2. Strategic design	– Selection of priority interaction groups, objective formulation, selection of communication modes/approaches
3. Development, pre-testing, production	– Design of messages and discussion themes, development of communication materials, pre-testing, review and modification of materials, production of materials
4. Management, implementation, monitoring	– Presentation of materials to all stakeholders; field staff training on the use of the communication materials; orientation of influential sources of information and advice; distribution of materials; implementation of communication approaches and activities; monitoring
5. Impact evaluation	- Gathering feedback from all priority interaction groups; evaluating the materials, analysis of the results; modification and re-printing.

2.2.1 Analysis

Existing literature on theories as well as studies on similar cases was examined. The script was revised in light of current legal issues pertaining to the rights of widows. Pamphlets on the New Inheritance Law available from the Legal Resources Foundation (LRF) and the Zimbabwe Women

---

[63] The P model is adapted from Koniz-Booher (1999: 105f), while additional steps follow partially the framework suggested by Anyaegbunam et al (1998: 14f).

Lawyers Association (ZWLA) were reviewed. This suggested that changes of the Inheritance Act from 1997 and a focus on customary marriages should be at the core of script change in order to provide participants with the correct legal information when reporting a deceased's estate.

2.2.2 Strategic design

At a very early stage of the project, the future distributors of the supporting material were identified and assessed. Organisations/institutions that were already known to have successfully used *Neria* in the past, as well as organisations, which had not used the film within their programmes so far, were contacted and asked to complete an assessment questionnaire to ensure that

- they are using video at a grassroots level in representative areas all over Zimbabwe and have some experience in the use of audio-visual media,
- they are currently and continuously running education and training programmes that are gender-sensitive,
- they have the institutional capacity, resources and the aim to network with like-minded groups, will further disseminate information about the material and will identify other groups at grassroots level to continuously ensure the further spread of the material.

Distributing organisations/institutions assisted in

- providing the information on social changes of the original script,
- providing information for a support package that served their various needs at local level,
- distributing and promoting the material to ensure it would reach the people for whom it had been designed.

The 30 chosen groups were contacted every two months to inform them about the project progress or to arrange pre-tests or training for trainers' workshops.

A design team of experts to oversee the development of the supporting material was formed to ensure that issues concerning the development of the material were supervised in a professional manner. The selection process of the design team members was based on their experience and knowledge in fields crucial to the development and distribution of the materials such as legal research, law, gender training, community education, women empowerment and sociology. The members participated in two design team meetings (May 2000; January 2001) and reviewed the concept paper, the research plan, and suggestions on script changes, research findings, draft scripts, the final draft video script and workbook.

2.2.3 Development, pre-testing and production

Formative participatory research to identify distributor groups' ideas about the *Neria* support material was conducted between August and October 2000 by making use of screenings and focus group discussions with groups of the distributors on the one hand and NGO personnel/resource persons on the other. Participants suggested the content and style of the material (which scenes should - in their opinion - be chosen for the support video and what should be incorporated in the manual). Having analysed the research findings, the expert group met to review the findings and to design a draft of the support materials.

The following is a summary of findings that led to the development of the supporting material, while, at the same time, providing a rich insight into perceptions, beliefs and inheritance practices supported by audience members.

2.2.3.1 Comments on characters

Comments on characters were both direct and indirect, on characters that enabled or hindered identification.

Neria was the character that received most (61) as well as most positive comments (37). She was perceived to be brave, strong, courageous, caring, humble and honest - a role model for Zimbabwean women. She respected tradition, but was at the same time self-reliant, a combination that many participants found worth striving for in their lives. While 11 comments found exactly these traits negative or unrealistic, 13 comments suggested that Neria should have looked for advice within her own or her husband's family first before discussing her problems with outsiders such as Connie or the co-operative women.

Patrick, the husband of Neria, received 18 comments, of which 16 were positive, stating that Patrick was a role model for Zimbabwean men. He was found to understand, to care for and to respect his immediate and extended family. People found he was a strong communicator who could discuss all issues with his wife and defend her against his own relatives. Two comments, however, found that he should have discussed even more with, especially, his relatives, since their action against Neria was triggered by a lack of understanding of the life he led with her in town.

Connie, the friend of Neria, was mentioned in 12 comments. Whilst seven of those were positive, acknowledging the friendship and good advice she gave to her friend, three were negative, dealing with her being too superstitious, which was found to be unrealistic. Two comments suggested that she should have respected the mourning period of her friend.

11 participants or groups mentioned Jethro, the brother of Neria. Only three comments were positive, acknowledging his brotherly care for Neria. However, six comments were negative, mainly because he kidnapped the 'kidnapped' son Shingayi without discussing it with Phineas. Others found that he did not support his sister as much as he could have. Two comments highlighted that Jethro could have controlled Phineas and so prevented Neria from suffering.

Sekuru, perceived by some to be the village elder, by others to be Ambuya's husband, was mentioned in five comments. Three were positive, acknowledging the support he offered in deciding to postpone the *kugara nhaka* ceremony. The other two were suggestions that dealt with his appropriate behaviour during the property distribution scene.

Mavis and Shingayi, the children of Neria and Patrick, received seven comments. Three of those were positive, having managed to portray realistically how children suffer from inheritance-related disputes. Two comments, however, found their behaviour unrealistic in that they never asked what had happened to their father. The two suggestions also found the children should have shown more emotional reaction to the death of their father.

As far as negative characters are concerned, Phineas, Patrick's elder brother, received as many as 35 comments of which only three were positive. Those dealt with his being honest and concerned. It was mentioned in Chapter I that resistance effects can play an important role in message reception processes. This result is actually a good example of this effect. Phineas usually got a lot of support from males when he was seen dancing with a prostitute or enjoying the fruits of someone else's labour. Those males were moreover disappointed with the film's outcome:

"It was not fair the way he was left out in the inheritance process" (male elder, Chishawasha, 2000),

"I do not agree with the film's outcome. Phineas is a very concerned guy. He says the truth. The way he behaves is how men behave in our culture. We have these rights and women are supposed to accept that" (male youngster, Gweru, 2000).

However, negative comments were in the majority. 20 participants or groups found him jealous, egoistic, lazy, greedy, oppressive, rude, ungrateful, lustful and careless about the children. 12 comments suggested that he should have been charged with theft or should have been shown to contract HIV/AIDS as a 'just punishment for his mean behaviour'.

Ambuya, Neria's mother-in law, was mentioned in 20 comments of which only two were positive. It was found that her change during the film and her support for Neria at the end was a role model for Zimbabwean mothers-in-law. However, thirteen comments perceived her to be a negative character in that her change was not found to be genuine. Her arguing with Neria was also found to be negative in that it caused unnecessary problems for all family members. Five suggestions dealt with her lack of support and her traditional role, which she neglected. She was found to be quiet or literally not present whenever she should have offered assistance.

11 comments were made about Maria, the wife of Phineas. None of them was positive. Eight comments found that Maria was too passive in accepting Phineas' behaviour, careless about the children of Neria and Patrick, as well as too greedy for the property of her sister-in-law. Some found her role unclear. However, three comments suggested that she should have resisted and refused the plans of her husband Phineas.

Joel, Patrick's eldest brother from Malawi, was mentioned in six comments. There were no positive and no clear negative comments, but the suggestions pointed out that he could have been a role model but was not, due to his lack of support for Neria and the family.

The women from the co-operative, the lawyers or the judge were not commented on directly, but were mentioned in combination with specific situations. The co-operative women were identified with support, skills for self-reliance and women's empowerment in 26 comments. The Judge was perceived to be a fair ruler, but as many as 14 comments found his sex or race a problem and a barrier to identification. While Mr. Chigwanzi, Phineas' lawyer, was commented on in connection with the court hearing, where eight comments found him to be too harsh on Neria and two comments to be too kind, Mr. Machacha, Neria's lawyer, received 12 positive comments as being a trustworthy and honest lawyer who defended her interests well in the court and who managed to reveal the egoistic motives of Phineas.

Tendai, the younger brother of Patrick, was mentioned indirectly by all 27 groups in connection with Phineas' proposal to Neria. It was felt that, according to custom, he should have proposed to Neria, as only the younger brother of the deceased can propose to his widow.

Neria's mother, who had appeared briefly, was not recognised by any of the viewers. 16 comments dealt with her non-existence and the supportive role she should have played in the film, suggesting that Neria's suffering could have been ended by the intervention of her blood relatives.

What transpires from these findings is that apparently, if liked, positive features of the source were noticed and produced positive cognitive responses, if disliked, negative features were noticed.

2.2.3.2 Awareness, attitudes and knowledge about state law and courts

Although most groups seemed to be aware of the Laws of Inheritance and the courts as a support system, ten groups asked for thorough information about procedures leading to property recovery. The general impression gained was that people did not know the exact contents of the laws and to whom which laws applied. Numerous questions, asked after the screenings of the unchanged film, reflect this. These questions resulted in the urge to get access to information about benefits for different marriage types, as well as procedures needed to formalise one's marriage uttered by as many as 20 out of 27 groups.

As far as attitudes about the law and the courts are concerned, the response was mixed. Positive comments on the Laws of Inheritance were obtained from nine groups, explaining that in Neria's particular situation, the law was the only remedy and the decision of the court was just. The idea that courts are protecting women was found to be positive. However, female participants from eight groups were concerned that they might not be in a position to pay for services when reporting an estate. They furthermore expressed concern about the consequences of making use of the Laws of Inheritance (such as tension arising in a village after challenging a brother-in-law or fighting him in court).

However, a great number of negative comments from 10 groups were uttered mainly by men, in connection with the Laws of Inheritance as amended by the government. The idea that the laws (Roman Dutch Law) were overcoming traditional law - thereby eroding the rights of Africans - was mentioned by half of the groups. Others saw the education about laws as the main source of change in society, which had, so they stated, negative consequences for men. They also complained about the type of support extended to widows.

Some women in urban areas noted that courts should not be promoted as support system to people based in rural areas, since customary support systems such as chiefs, elders and traditional healers were of greater importance to such target group.

2.2.3.3 Indigenous inheritance customs and practices

Triggered by the practices seen in the film, audience members felt the need to describe their own indigenous customs and practices. In order to get an accurate description, people usually referred to elders - male as well as female - in the audience. Elders of eight groups did not agree with the time, the way and the beneficiaries of the property distribution. That the property was given to the widow in the film was, although appreciated during the screening of the film, criticised later and considered to not be a part of one's culture. Dependants/relatives (such as mother-in-law and father-in-law on both sides), as it was uttered clearly by 10 groups, needed be to honoured by allocating them property shares. Five groups described the property distribution itself as a friendly, negotiated meeting where the widow also had a say, unlike in the film.

When people started to discuss their indigenous inheritance customs, as they were carried out long ago or are still carried out today, the idea that widow inheritance was not forced was central to the discussions. In 20 out of 27 groups, the topic was discussed heatedly as to the correct procedure and appropriateness of *kugara nhaka*. While some agreed that a widow had the chance to refuse a remarriage (by choosing her child during the ceremony), there was at the same time the belief and the practice that a widow could not stay at her deceased husband's place on her own. She was supposed to move away when choosing not to remarry. This, so it was said, was necessary to prevent boyfriends (that a widow would ultimately have) to stay at the place of the deceased. Since it was believed that a woman would have boyfriends anyway, a common comment was that

"I prefer widow inheritance so the daughter-in-law will stay in the village where she can be monitored" (excerpt from a focus group discussion with a mixed group of community members, Muzokomba 2000).

All 20 groups suggested that when the child was chosen, he should have definitely passed on the sticks to his father's younger brother as a *sara pavana*, as the child needed support from his father's family until grown up. However, as a practice, widow inheritance was criticised mainly by women and church groups, as it was found to be - provoked by greed and a lack of respect for the deceased relative - a source of women's oppression, illnesses and death. Others pointed out that, originally, widow inheritance was a good practice to look after the widow and the children of the deceased and not to sleep with her anyway. However, the majority of 14 groups were willing to discuss the issue and to consider the different arguments.

2.2.3.4 Property grabbing

Women from 11 groups stated that property grabbing was not only happening to them frequently, but also to men. In most cases it was believed that the property grabbers were somehow involved in the death of their relative. A strong need for information as to which procedures one can take to recover the property came out clearly. Members of 19 groups asked for advice or further information. Explanations for the prevalence of property grabbing from eight groups ranged from justifications for revenge, due to unpaid *lobola*, or the neglect of elders' advice when getting married, to the observed need to control a daughter-in-law who is interested in remarrying outside the family. Others mentioned that property grabbing had nothing to do with Customary Law and was done out of sheer greed.

2.2.3.5 Property distribution and property registration

How should the property of the deceased[64] be distributed? A majority of 17 groups out of 27 groups suggested the widow to be the main beneficiary in order to look after the children.

"I learnt that when the brother was still alive, he was communicating nicely with his wife. The elder brother was always complaining. So, as men, we should learn that we give the property rather to the family than to the relatives" (excerpt from a focus group discussion with a mixed group of caregivers, Kwekwe 2000).

11 groups mentioned some concerns as to whether women were capable of looking after the children after being allocated the wealth. Although the consensus was that women were most fit to look after the family, it was mentioned that some women were greedy and neglected the children when the wealth was used up.

---

[64] The 'property of the deceased' is in most cases the joint property of the immediate family. People refer to the property of the deceased when talking about a deceased male (to which they refer in most cases) and do hereby include all the property of the wife except *mawoko*. So if the wife has contributed through monetary and other means and if, say half of what makes up this property was bought with her money but for the family, then again it is referred to as the property of the deceased, which she might be deprived of.

The other groups nominated children to be the main beneficiaries in order to counter this perceived abuse. This referred to children born in and out of wedlock alike.

2.2.3.6 Wills

Triggered by the viewing of *Neria*, the majority of groups started to discuss freely about wills. Wills, so was stated by as many as 19 groups, needed to be written down to prevent the immediate family from such problems shown in the film. Although people admitted that wills could attract bad luck (by making arrangements for one's own death), they saw, through the film's example that writing down one's wishes can counter problems. People understood further that wills could be written not only by men but also by women. However, when probing as to what needed to be in a will to make it valid, all participants, except the legal support groups, admitted they needed further information on the issue.

2.2.3.7 Witchcraft

The film portrayed a number of issues related to witchcraft, which triggered discussion in as many as 15 groups. It was said that witchcraft existed in everyday lives and that beliefs in superstition also helped to counter irregularities.

"Before Patrick died, we realised that the ball was kicked to the window, we saw the snake or the water pot breaking, that actually shows that the superstitions indicated something terrible was going to happen. Certain signs are part of our African everyday life. They can mean that either something was going to happen naturally or someone was doing a bad thing. We do have these signs just like a bee near you to show you maybe you are expecting a visitor" (excerpt from a focus group discussion with a mixed group of community members, Chishawasha 2000).

2.2.3.8 The relationship between the immediate and the extended family

Triggered by the presentation of a harmonious relationship on the one side and greedy, interfering relatives on the other, as many as 19 groups mentioned that the immediate family has its own life to lead and that extended family members should not interfere with this life. Other statements were made concerning the ideal relationship between husband and wife such as 'couples should pool resources and discuss all issues together' (mentioned by 13 groups) and 'men should be able to assist women with all problems they face' (mentioned by nine groups). However, 16 groups found that troubles usually originate from the town-rural area clash and the refusal of children to inform their parents and other relatives once they have moved to town. Therefore, people suggested that the extended family needed to be informed and all current issues should be discussed once in a while.

"We are in town, nobody would like to stay in the rural areas forever. If you work in town, you can develop the rural areas better, but since we are so busy, we do neglect our rural folk. When we need something from them, they do not understand us. This reflects in the scene Patrick-Ambuya. We should go back to the rural areas on a regular basis and explain to children and elders. They will appreciate what I am doing in town as long as I do see them regularly. Moreover, they should come to town, too, to understand and enjoy" (excerpt from a focus group discussion with a group of HIV/AIDS activists, Gweru 2000).

The extended family, so they suggested, played such an important role in the lives of the immediate family members that one needed to stay "in good books" with them.

2.2.3.9 Film impact

18 groups mentioned that the film was very relevant in both the urban and the rural areas and portrayed what was really happening. 12 groups found the gender issues in combination with inheritance practices extremely suitable to trigger the questioning of attitudes held towards these issues. According to 11 groups, the film taught about African life as well as new issues, while seven groups felt the film gave inspiration to share information with others. Then, the manifold discussions, created through the film, led a number of groups to appreciate the film and the medium that triggered them.

"The film as it stands is a really good film. I think it deserves to fetch more prizes again because it provokes all these discussions we are having" (Focus group discussion with a mixed group of traditional healers, Harare 2000).

2.2.3.10 Problems participants face and support participants need

People came up with a range of barriers that needed to be overcome in order to access inheritance-related benefits. Graph 2 below reflects these. The need for thorough information was mentioned by all 27 groups: information regarding not only the Laws of Inheritance but also how co-operatives can be formed, this being requested by eight groups. Asked how this information should be transmitted, the majority (19 groups) voted for a reintroduction of mobile cinemas to show the *Neria* film and other films that provide information on issues of social relevance. Ten groups mentioned that when making use of mobile film units, brochures should be handed out at the same time 'to take the information home to others who could not attend'. Seven groups favoured radio lessons in vernacular languages or mentioned programmes or activities from NGOs.

Graph 2 – Problems faced when wanting to access inheritance benefits

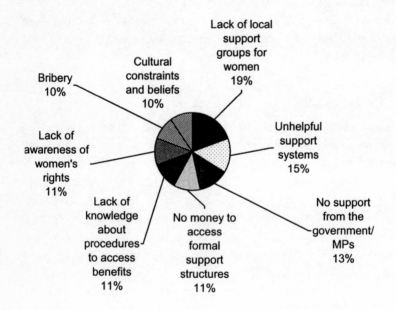

When asked who should be provided with this type of information, 23 groups preferred it to be brought to women and men together. Two groups felt women's groups should be given priority, while two groups felt that the focus should be specifically on the education of children.

2.2.3.11   How was the material designed? A summary

Judging from the information participants provided as well as the questions they raised above, the *Neria* supporting material should focus on the main learning points raised in the feature film, should pose questions in a thought-provoking way, should be designed to encourage discussion, should deepen the knowledge provided in the film and should stimulate target groups to revise their existing attitudes on women's issues to facilitate an empowering process. Together with the feature film, the material should serve as powerful interactive tools, but would at the same time be designed in such a manner as to be used as independent learning tools.

The support video made use of 22 scenes from the feature film within 24 minutes. Those scenes were grouped into six sequences. Four different characters from the film narrated the main issues raised in the film. This was done in a thought-provoking way in order to allow the viewer to discover her or his own possibilities for decision-making processes - as opposed to providing pre-conceived solutions. The following main sequences were created:

Sequence 1 - Culture

Sequence 2 – Traditional values in a changing society

A.: Immediate family

B.: Extended family

Sequence 3 – Abuse of tradition; twisting tradition

A.: Greed; neglect from the extended family

B.: STDs; HIV/AIDS

C.: Domestic violence

D.: Child neglect; child abuse; orphans

E.: Witchcraft; superstition

Sequence 4 – Informal support systems

A.: Support from the women's co-operative; support from friends

B.: Savings account; registration of property

C.: Extended family support
Sequence 5 – Formal support systems
A.: Law
B.: Marriage; wills
C.: Property distribution
D.: Going to court
E.: Guardianship; custody
F.: Life insurance; pensions
G.: Constraints you might face
Sequence 6 – Culture and change

To allow structured discussion when using the video, fade-outs were inserted after each sequence to pause for discussion.

The support manual was designed to facilitate the use of the film and the video in a joint session, but should also be used on its own where video facilities were not available. It was structured along the themes listed above. The design process focused mainly on

- Deepening the knowledge of issues raised in the film/video,
- encouraging group work and discussions as well as
- supporting the creativity of participants to think about solutions to their own problems within their own communities and social groups.

Taking into consideration the target beneficiaries of the package, the manual was designed to be

- Easy to read,
- compiled in the major local languages Shona, Ndebele and English,
- accompanied by six picture cards (one for each sequence) when video is not available,
- accompanied by three Legal Resources Foundation (LRF) brochures that provide facts on inheritance procedures and the writing of wills and an address list of all distributors and legal support groups located in all provinces of Zimbabwe.

Research to pre-test the supporting material was carried out between March and May 2001. As far as understanding the content of the video is concerned, rural audiences who had not seen the film before found the story (in particular, story details) unclear, although the overall message was under-

stood. Some mentioned that 20 minutes seemed to be too short to familiar-
ise with the characters, names, questions and solutions offered. Other audiences, especially in Ndebele speaking areas, found the video very logical
and clear, although none of them had seen the feature film before. When
looking at the effective use of the video, people could remember well what
they had seen in each sequence, especially in cases where the tape was
shown in sections with discussions. Messages that participants understood
are summarised below (Graph 3). What the narration clearly stimulated was
discussion on how customs were carried out long back, why they were
changed, what can be done and who should be a responsible agent of
change.

Graph 3 – Messages understood by pre-test participants

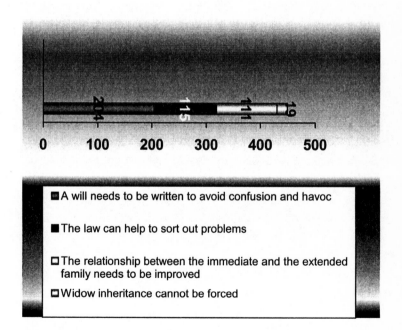

109

When people tested the arrangement of the support manual, they found it very logical and clear. As far as the content is concerned, all the subjects raised in the manual were found to be appropriate and useful. A number of questions had to be reformulated or cut out since the wording was found to be inaccurate, confusing or questions were considered to be too open (such as taboo issues dealing with domestic violence or HIV/AIDS). It was furthermore not found to be adequately mentioned how the discussion could be facilitated. However, the manual was rated a useful educational tool to guide and focus discussion, to raise awareness and to provide further information. The accompanying legal educational pamphlets were found to be of invaluable help to people especially in remoter areas.

After the review, the final documents were designed. From July to August 2001, the support manual and the video sleeves were now translated and the material was printed. 300 sets[65] were prepared to be distributed free of charge to the chosen groups.

2.3 The grassroots distribution campaign

In order to distribute the newly designed audio-visual material, the following main tasks were carried out.

2.3.1 Management, implementation and monitoring

Between July and September 2001, the Training for Trainers' workshops' agendas were designed, facilitators and venues were chosen. In September 2001, two two-day Training for Trainers' workshops were held in Harare and Bulawayo. The following issues were discussed during both workshops:

- Expectations and fears concerning the workshops and the role of a distributor,
- The *Neria* project (objectives and limitations),
- Communication for development (definition, barriers, strategies, video),

---

[65] Note that one set includes one VHS *Neria* feature film, one VHS *Neria* support video and one *Neria* support manual.

- Inheritance. Discussing the issues raised in *Neria* and how they affect communities with which they work,
- Technical aspects - the role of a distributor (requirements and tasks),
- Inheritance. The new laws and their benefits (eight pieces of legislation),
- The *Neria* support material. Suggestions for the use (discussing the manual with the video and the picture cards),
- Planning effective distribution strategies in the communities (how to mainstream or incorporate the *Neria* project into existing programmes, how to promote and distribute the materials and how to form strategic alliances with other organisations already in the field).

One member of each distributor's organisation or institution received training in the use of the support package. Participants had to come up with an action plan on how they were going to promote the availability of the material. After they were supplied with a number of sets (according to their needs), they independently started to distribute their sets through their networks (free lending, donations, education programmes or sales). To facilitate a wide spread of the support package, the revised and dubbed versions of the *Neria* feature film were broadcast on national television (Ndebele in November 2001, Shona in March 2002). National newspapers, magazines and organisations' newsletters published information on the availability of the material. This was carried out to serve a wide spread of the new film's messages and was meant at the same time to promote the availability of the support package in urban and rural areas. Through the careful choice of distributors and the participative manner of the project it was intended to support already set-up structures and activate at the same time local initiatives for the empowerment of the beneficiaries. After six months to one year, the distributors provided MFD with progress reports on how the package was being used and which obstacles were being faced in the process. Comments are summarised below.

2.3.2 Distributors' feedback and impact evaluation

After the programme had been running for 12 months, MFD had received reports from 17 out of 30 groups. Reasons for the failure of the other 13 groups to provide feedback originated mainly from harsh economic conditions that affected all programmes implemented and resulted occasionally in a total withdrawal from the field, in the change of contact persons who were usually not familiar with what had been agreed with colleagues, or lack of interest. However, the 17 groups have provided substantial feedback on the use and promotion of the materials, on participants' responses as well as on the impact of the materials all of which will be described below.

2.3.2.1   Use and promotion of support materials by distributors

The *Neria* distributors mentioned that the material was incorporated into HIV/AIDS programmes for male youth, it was shown to local leaders and to domestic violence victims and it was used in Training for Trainers' seminars and in programmes concerning family awareness:

"Every month, a one day workshop has been held to reveal to the participants the holistic need of a will in a family structure. In all these symposiums the participants clearly indicated the detrimental effects of living behind your loved ones without a will that will safeguard their future; special emphasis who when parents die in testate are left with absolutely nothing as all the property is taken by relatives" (excerpt from the report of a Catholic church-based network to eradicate HIV/AIDS, 2001).

Neria was moreover shown to home-based care participants, it was used in church groups or it was shown to local leaders during district development meetings.

"We organised a workshop which was attended by the local leaders, elders of the community and project participants addressing the issue of inheritance in the traditional way and modern ways taking into account the government's current act on inheritance. During this workshop the Neria Shona clip was shown and booklets were distributed. We are very keen to disseminate the information in the future" (excerpt from the report of a training centre that focuses on practical skills, 2001).

Networking, co-operation and facilitation links were created, which not only included members from other *Neria* support groups, but also extended to the invitation of external experts to supplement the programme.

"We invited a lawyer to give an afternoon to the ladies and try to identify the real problem. This was highly appreciated. Attitudes take time to alter. We understand and accept the people around us here and patiently continue looking for meaningful ways of helping this change of attitude" (excerpt from the report of a church-based disaster relief group, 2001).

Networks were established in order to carry out exchange visits, sharing reports, continuing meetings and loaning the materials to key organisations.

"The packages that we did receive of *Neria*, English and vernacular, have gone a long way in enhancing conceptualisation of the message embedded in the video clip....I took the initiative to discuss with various Ministries and other organisations notifying them of this free consignment. Public places had posters on free space to enable those who would want to access the video to be at their disposal. A detailed register was put in place that reflects video borrowing activities" (excerpt from the report of a rural development association, 2002).

2.3.2.2 Participants' responses

Participants' feedback on the package was mixed. While one group experienced problems with men being slow to respond to the video activity, the youth, so it seemed, reacted more positively.

"From the youths, the general feeling was that they were getting equipped to be able to face challenges should these arise later in life. They felt that the video got them empowered on decision making skills and the ability to support each other with constructive ideas especially among girl youths" (excerpt from a report of an HIV/AIDS activist group, 2001).

Constraints when using the film in attitude and awareness change programmes were also reported.

"The effect of *Neria* on women and widows has been very unsatisfactory – our community in Chipinge is very much culture-bound. Women are not free to discuss matters of inheritance and our efforts are yielding very little results. The ordinary woman in Chipinge sees culture as it stands today as a protective weapon – even to talk about property grabbing as a social problem seems to go against the culture. Trying to understand the thinking system and perception of these cultural activities around our women here needs a lot of time and intensive education. A year is not enough. Reporting becomes impossible, because the effect is not yet felt. We could give you numbers of those who have watched the videos but what is numbers when it comes to community sensitisation" (excerpt from the report of a church-based charity group, 2002).

These mere cultural constraints were also identified in many other parts of the country,

"Indeed, the majority of our populace and Zimbabwe at large is still hiding behind the words 'Traditions' and 'Customs' of which they do not really know the prac-

113

tices; in the process wives and children are not safeguarded" (excerpt from the report of a Catholic church-based network to eradicate HIV/AIDS, 2001),

but it did not hinder the implementation of the programme nor did participants react slowly, as the following comment suggests.

"The participants of the workshops appreciated the programme as "an eye opener for the wrong conception that existed about the will". They also acknowledged the programme as something that facilitated communication between husbands and wives, the immediate and extended families and the entire community on matters regarding property rights. A great number of the participants openly argued that if such a programme is facilitated at such a macro level as the diocese, the plight and suffering of orphans may be reduced" (excerpt from the report of a Catholic church-based network to eradicate HIV/AIDS, 2001).

In fact, most groups reported a positive feedback from their participants.

"Women need to know the options available to them when faced with Neria's situation. It empowers them to see a woman like them being able to conquer such a situation. The film relates to what most women can identify within their daily lives. Most of our members are in rural areas where other forms of media are scarce" (excerpt from the report of a skills training group for women and girls, 2001).

"Our constituent members happen to be the target group of the film because of residing in the rural communities where norms and cultural beliefs still shape and design the majority of people's lives. Furthermore inheritance-related problems are significantly abundant in the rural areas. When using the film we have experienced a breakthrough especially with traditionalists. While at first, they did not know how to relate to the shown issues personally, as the film went on, they suddenly realised it was dealing with their beliefs and norms and how those can cause problems for other community members" (excerpt from a rural development association, 2001).

As a way forward, other groups have identified the following strategies:

- To identify more widows to see the video,
- the need to empower women on decision-making skills,
- to show the video in rural schools,
- to organise workshops for local decision-makers.

114

2.3.2.3   Impact of the material

Distributing groups suggested that the material had a great impact on their communities, because people were encouraged to learn in the vernacular and were prepared to share knowledge with each other. Others mentioned that the viewing of the film in mixed groups facilitated discussion with people discarding unfashionable practices. Another crucial point was the finding that visual images had a lasting impact and were a basis for discussion. It was reported that people seemed to learn from what they saw, and talked about, and from the characters with which they empathised and identified.

However, it was also realistically pointed out that a long-term impact could only be achieved if the programme was ongoing with adequate resources, and with systems and structures set up at community level (community ownership).

How the *Neria* material was further distributed in a multi-media awareness campaign and how it was perceived by beneficiaries will be described below.

3   The Wills and Inheritance Laws Campaign

The distribution and the use of the *Neria* support material in the context of a multimedia educational inheritance campaign implemented by the Zimbabwean Ministry of Justice, Legal and Parliamentary Affairs will be explored below.

3.1   Background

As described in the preceding chapter MFD has dubbed *Neria* into Shona and Ndebele and developed educational support material for the film in 2000/2001 (see also Karikoga 2001 or Moyo 2001). When this material was in the pre-testing stage, the Wills and Inheritance Programme was launched and forces were joined to increase the impact of *Neria* on audiences throughout Zimbabwe.

3.2 The campaign - objectives and activities

The Wills and Inheritance Laws Programme was a multi-media campaign aimed at raising awareness concerning the Zimbabwean Laws of Inheritance and encouraging their use. It was a programme initiated by the Zimbabwean Ministry of Justice, Legal and Parliamentary Affairs and was managed by Africa Community Communications (Africcomms).

Objectives were

- To ensure that, on the death of a person, the surviving spouse, dependants and orphans can access and utilise the inheritance laws of the country,

- To ensure equity in the distribution of assets to surviving spouses, dependants and orphans,

- To encourage individuals in the making of wills so that they can avoid the problems related to in testate succession,

- To reach as many people as possible through the media campaign, using a number of channels such as radio, video and community drama,

- To train secondary stakeholders, especially within the court system and traditional leaders, to build their capacity to support communities to access and use inheritance and wills laws,

- To create greater knowledge of the laws relating to inheritance (K2 Techno Consult 2001: 4).

The goal of the multi-media communication campaign was to ensure equity in the distribution of assets to surviving spouses and dependants to prevent suffering. Table 4 below describes the activities implemented in the course of the campaign. In order to co-ordinate all these efforts, regular meetings with working group members (a total of 29 chosen Zimbabwean organisations) and stakeholder workshops were held in the course of the 18 months' campaign.

4 *Neria* as part of the Wills and Inheritance Laws Programme

"The 1992 Zimbabwean film *Neria*, which explores modern approaches to overcoming traditional practices that oppress women, has prompted a debate on the use of film and video in mass education campaigns (...). Many women's groups, in Zimbabwe and abroad, are currently considering how the film can be used to educate women on their legal rights, as the film touches on issues of inheritance and family law" (UNICEF 1994: 44). In order to facilitate the use of film and video within this mass educational campaign, MFD was contracted to contribute to the section of material development, which was mainly preoccupied with adapting

"socio-culturally relevant and appropriate audio-visual information, education and communication material for use in interpersonal and group learning with rural and urban communities" (K2 Techtop Consult 2001: 5).

Table 4 – Campaign activities

Field	Activity
Research	- National participatory rural and urban communication appraisal, - National awareness, knowledge, attitudes and practices baseline survey based on the appraisal's findings, - Projects communications strategy, - Project monitoring and evaluation strategy,
Material development	- Video and supporting material, - Cartoons, stickers, - Trainers' manual,
Theatre	- National theatre for development programme,
Television	- Television spots, four week talk show, 52 week series social soap opera,
Radio	- Radio spots, four week talk show, 52 week series radio drama,
CD	- 10 track CD with Zimbabwean musicians,
Training	- Training of community facilitators and NGO users of all audio-visual material of the campaign, - 57 district workshops for district, ward and village campaign facilitators,
Legal Aid	- Provision of legal aid and assistance to members of the public who need assistance as a result of campaign activities.

The material should address gaps in awareness, knowledge, attitudes and practices amongst disadvantaged urban and rural communities. The project was called '*Neria* Communication Kit'.

4.1 Objectives and activities of the project

The *Neria* communication kit project had the following *objectives*:
- To focus on gaps in awareness, knowledge, attitude and practices for urban and rural learners,
- To ensure that socially relevant issues in connection with inheritance are addressed,
- To promote gender and awareness on inheritance-related issues amongst communities in Zimbabwe.

It sought to address these by carrying out the following *activities*:
- To brand the recently developed *Neria* material for the Wills and Inheritance Laws Programme, thereby adapting it to the campaign's goals (such as the creation of new master tapes for logo and text insertion or the design of stickers to brand written material),
- To produce 156 *Neria* sets (the '*Neria* communication kit') for the campaign.

4.2 Production of materials

The '*Neria* Communication Kit Programme' was finally implemented in November 2001. Pre-campaign studies (Moetsabi 2001: 9-44; see also Ruzvidzo, Tichagwa 2001; K2 Techtop Consult 2001 or RSC Zimbabwe 2001) were reviewed, videotexts of the feature film and the support video were redesigned and translated and the campaign logo as well as the branding text was inserted. To complement the communication kit, *Neria* posters were included.

4.3 Video distribution through road shows and Ladies' Clubs

MFD's main aim in the campaign was to transmit information to audiences who have not had access beforehand and to raise awareness on issues brought up in *Neria*. This was facilitated by the International Video Fair

(IVF)[66], a group that promotes education through video in Southern Africa. They offered to screen the *Neria* video in remote areas of Zimbabwe by engaging Experiential Momentum for this task. This is a group of marketing experts, who use traditional teaching methods combined with new technologies to promote their clients' products. Experiential Momentum has a number of trucks equipped with a stage and a bioscope. They take programmes of different clients (such as UniLever, PSI or New Start Centre)[67] to any growth point in Zimbabwe. When promoting the programmes, Experiential Momentum utilises drama, question and answer sessions and songs in vernacular languages. They usually attract large crowds and their shows represent a reliable way of getting the message to as many people as possible in areas where there is no electricity or people usually have no access to television, radio or newspapers.

It was finally agreed to present *Neria* as part of the Wills and Inheritance Laws Programme in the following format:

- Creating a one hour Wills and Inheritance Laws session for road shows (using talks and an inheritance quiz before showing the *Neria* support video in either Shona or Ndebele every day on their tour for the following six months) and

- Informing, especially women, in set-up 'Ladies' Clubs (which are established groups in all provinces of Zimbabwe, who usually gather once a week to discuss issues of clients' products as well as issues of social importance) about the new Laws of Inheritance and organising screen-

---

[66] The International Video Fair (IVF) is an initiative that aims at disseminating information regarding development issues through the use of video. Audiences they screen to are usually at the bottom of the list in terms of their access to education on critical social and development issues. It is generally these audiences, so IVF, that are also the most vulnerable to the maladies of these development issues. It is IVF's vision to educate these communities on issues that are of the greatest importance to their lives. Screenings IVF conducts are free of charge. Screening programmes run throughout the year, revisiting areas every few months in order to ensure long-term impact and follow-up programming. IVF screens videos that are exclusively made in Africa.

[67] PSI is a Zimbabwean NGO engaged in creating HIV/AIDS awareness and New Start Centres are subsidised HIV/AIDS counselling and testing centres all over Zimbabwe.

ings of the *Neria* support video or feature film together with the manual in the households of group leaders.

Trained staff was organised to be on hand to answer questions the audience might have. This formula of combining screenings, discussions and the handing out of information packages has proved to be an effective way of disseminating information. Both programmes were implemented from May 2002 through to October 2002. Through this combined programme, Experiential Momentum could reach 357 800 road show viewers and 15 597 Ladies' Clubs' viewers throughout Zimbabwe. How those viewers perceived the programme and in specific, the *Neria* support material, will be explored in the following chapter.

Chapter V
Analysis of Wills and Inheritance Laws Programme participants' responses

1 The *Neria* questionnaire exercise

In order to capture participants' and trainers' ideas about the *Neria* communication kit during the campaign, questionnaires (see Appendix 2.3) were designed by the author, were translated into Shona and Ndebele and distributed by the road show crew, who was briefed on the forms during an afternoon session. This briefing aimed at summarising the information on the Laws of Inheritance and at highlighting the need to recommend the use of support services to participants after each screening. Experiential Momentum crew was instructed to use six forms randomly during each road show screening and to leave a number of forms with each Ladies' Club team leader. Results are listed and analysed in this chapter.

The *Neria* questionnaires were completed by
- Screening participants who were exposed to a 30-minute information session, a quiz on the Laws of Inheritance and a vernacular version of the *Neria* support video in a large mixed crowd. After watching the film, they filled in the questionnaire. These participants will be referred to as Group 1 or Road show Group in the following,
- Screening participants who were exposed to a 30-minute information session, the screening of a vernacular version of the *Neria* feature film or support video and the use of the support material (manual and support video) in a discussion group. Having seen the film and having participated in a discussion, they filled in the questionnaire. All participants were female and the groups were already established. These participants will be called Group 2 or Ladies' Clubs in the following, and finally
- Participants who were exposed to a 30-minute information session and a group discussion only. No film was shown. After the discussion, a

slightly altered[68] questionnaire was filled in. All participants were female and the groups were already established. These participants will be referred to as Group 3 or Ladies' Clubs 2 in the following.

A total of 524 road show forms (443 Shona forms and 78 Ndebele forms) and a total of 720 Ladies' Clubs' forms (360 Shona forms and 360 Ndebele forms) were completed and returned to MFD[69]. Where they were filled in and by who can be seen below.

1.1 Date and venue

Experiential Momentum field-tested the *Neria* video from May 2002 through to September 2002 and promoted the Laws of Inheritance during 93 road shows in most provinces of Zimbabwe. The programme joined the road show circuit while it was already operating with a fixed route list, which, for these five months, consisted mainly of Shona speaking areas. Whilst they visited 59 locations in rural areas and 34 locations in urban or semi-urban areas, only 14 of them were in Matabeleland. For this reason, Shona and Ndebele road show results were combined in this analysis. The Laws of Inheritance were promoted during 448 Ladies' Clubs' meetings, but the analysis was carried out in 60 meetings, 30 of each in Shona and Ndebele speaking areas. All Ladies' Clubs' meetings took place in urban or semi-urban high-density areas.

---

[68] Since Group 3 members had not seen the film, they commented on the inheritance session instead.

[69] Note that the actual number of forms received was higher, but had to be reduced for a number of reasons. Spoilt forms (forms that gave reason to believe that the answers did not come from the audience but from road show crewmembers. The same answer was, for example, given with exactly the same words for four locations in a row, which is practically impossible) were discovered in June 2002. After a meeting with the responsible individuals, it became clear that people needed incentives for the inheritance quiz and to fill in the forms after the show, so it was decided to provide *Neria* videos, posters, inheritance caps, *Neria* manuals and pamphlets. From then on, the quality of the forms improved.

1.2 Audience numbers and type

During the road show programme from May to September 2002, a total of 352 600 road show viewers could be counted throughout Zimbabwe. As Graph 4 below shows, the road show attendance figures increased gradually with the months - a fact that can be attributed to a more relaxed political climate after the presidential elections but also to an increased interest in the Wills and Inheritance Laws Programme and the film *Neria*[70]. Road show crewmembers reported that the actual audience figures were counted before the film started, since this was when the daily audience numbers were the highest. The information session on the Laws of Inheritance usually started half an hour before the film.

Graph 4 – Road show attendance

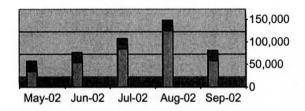

While a total of 352 600 road show viewers were present when the research was carried out, feedback was gained from a random selection of 524 road show viewers. Of the total of 524 valid road show forms returned, women filled in 248 of them, men filled in 276. With 59 rural and 34 urban venues, a slightly higher percentage of participants from low-income groups, particularly those from the rural areas, can be assumed.

During the Ladies' Clubs' programme, a total of 15 597 (Experiential Momentum 2002) Ladies' Clubs' viewers could be counted in four provinces of Zimbabwe. While 3 498 Ladies' Clubs' viewers were present when the

---

[70] The slight decline in September can be attributed to the fact that only half the number of shows planned was carried out due to technical problems of Experiential Momentum's screening vehicles.

research was carried out, a total of 720 forms were received (360 Shona forms and 360 Ndebele forms). Of these, 180 Shona and 180 Ndebele forms made up Group 2 and 180 Shona and 180 Ndebele forms made up Group 3. Group 2 consisted of 880 Harare-based viewers and 941 Bulawayo-based viewers. Group 3 consisted of 867 Harare-based participants and 765 Bulawayo-based participants.

During Ladies' Clubs' meetings that took place in the mornings only, existing Ladies' Clubs were informed about the Laws of Inheritance and were asked to group at places where video facilities were available. They watched the video and completed the forms. There was a special focus on the discussion aspect and Ladies' Clubs' sessions usually lasted between three and four hours for Group 2 and about two hours for Group 3. The age range of interview participants was between 30 and 60 years. All participants resided in either semi-urban or urban high-density areas. Low-income groups were prevalent. Participants were in most cases either self-employed in the informal sector or unemployed.

1.3   Formal educational level of questionnaire participants

Looking at the formal educational level of questionnaire participants by research groups, Graph 5 below shows that Grade 7 or Standard 6 was the highest educational level amongst participants of Group 1 and Group 3. The majority of Group 2 participants obtained O-levels, followed by Grade 7 or Standard 6. 'No formal schooling' was quite common in all three groups but highest in Group 3. A-levels and university degrees were not obtained by members of Group 2 and 3, but by a minority of Group 1 participants. Looking at the male-female ratio and the urban-rural ratio in Group 1, it is interesting to note that 'no formal schooling' and Grade 7 or Standard 6 levels were considerably higher amongst rural road show participants and of those of female participants.

Looking at the formal educational level of questionnaire participants by sex, it becomes clear that women's levels were always lower than men's levels. This was enforced by the area of residence and - consequently - the degree of exposure to information and education. While rural men's highest educational level reached was Grade 7 or Standard 6, this was similar with rural women. However, the percentage of rural women who never went to school was slightly higher than the figure for their male counterparts. Urban men's highest formal educational level was the O-level while urban women's highest level was Grade 7 or Standard. 6. The highest number of participants with A-levels and/or university degrees could be found amongst urban men.

Looking at Group 2 and 3, which comprised female urban-based participants, O-level as well as Grade 7 or Standard 6 were prevalent. Group 3, however, had a higher percentage of participants who never went to school. When looking at all questionnaire respondents together, the majority of all participants attained Grade 7 or Standard 6, followed by O-levels and 'no formal schooling'. A-levels as well as university degrees were extremely rare.

Graph 5 – Formal educational level of questionnaire respondents

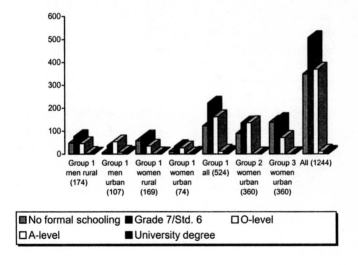

1.4 Age range of participants by groups

As far as the age range of questionnaire participants is concerned, 26-35 year old participants were in the majority amongst all groups. This was followed by 36-45 year olds in the road show group, and then 19-25 years olds amongst Ladies' Clubs' participants of Group 2 and 3. '46 and older' was better represented amongst the road show group, while 15-18 year olds were under-represented amongst all groups (see Graph 6 below). Looking at the sex and home location ratio, rural road show participants were generally well represented in both 26-35 as well as in the 36-45 range. Women were in both groups in the majority.

Graph 6 – Age range of questionnaire respondents by research group

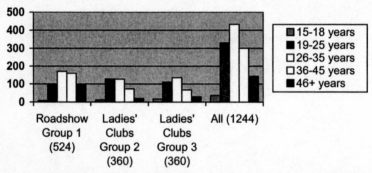

While the age range in the urban group and the rural group was similar, male participants were slightly in the majority (partly due to the time of the screening around 6 p.m., when more women were presumably engaged in household activities; partly due to cultural attitudes in some screening areas that negatively affected the attendance figures of women, see also Matewa 2002).

19-35 year olds are an important target group of the material, mainly because they are most likely to be affected by inheritance-related problems due to the HIV/AIDS pandemic.

2 Appropriateness of the supporting material

Participants of Group 2 were asked to describe their use of the *Neria* training package. 884 valid responses listed three options:

- Option 1 - An inheritance session in vernacular languages followed by the viewing of the support video and a discussion (approximately 90 minutes needed for the programme),

- Option 2 - An inheritance session in vernacular languages followed by the support video used together with the support manual/guided discussion (approximately 150 minutes needed for the programme),

- Option 3 - An inheritance session in vernacular languages followed by the screening of the feature film, followed by the screening of the support video and the use of the manual/guided discussion (approximately 240 minutes needed for the programme).

Amongst participants of Group 2, all three options were used equally (each 120 questionnaires were received from groups who had used one of the three options). Group 1, however, used Option 1 only, since the road show schedule did not allow for more than 90 minutes for the inheritance session, the film and the official discussion[71] (see Graph 7 below). Group 3 did not use any of the options.

Group 2 participants with Option 1 felt their time to discuss relevant sections of the video was not sufficient, while Option 2 participants felt satisfied. Option 3 participants however mentioned that their discussion was most fruitful, but a session as long as 240 minutes to discuss all issues was not realistic in a normal training set-up. Looking at the suitability of the questions in video and manual used by Group 2, answers reflected no significant difference for Shona and Ndebele groups. Those who tested Option 1 (no manual) in a support group set-up felt that the questions (from the video) helped, but they were not sufficient to get thorough information on a number of issues.

---

[71] Participants of Group 1 did not fill in this section, but their comments obtained in the recommendations section (see below) suggest that the support video was not really appropriate for large crowds without a follow-up or a discussion.

Graph 7 – The use of the training package - all groups

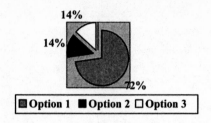

14%

14%

72%

| Option 1 | Option 2 | Option 3 |

Much more satisfied was the group with Option 2, who was using the manual, which helped them to understand the issues, get further information and which triggered guided discussion. Participants with Option 3 reported the highest information gain due to their use of three different tools as well as the sufficient time given to using these tools. The reported learning effect was highest amongst Option 3 participants, as manual questions assisted in learning about different issues, in providing information as well as in triggering discussion.

Asked whether the style of the material was appropriate for the target group, 86 percent of the three sub-segments of Group 2 (360) found it useful, while 14 percent liked the material but felt it was not very effective, mainly due to unclear wording and unclear scenes.

3   Effects of the supporting material on participants

The following eleven sections were derived from questionnaires filled in by participants of Group 1, 2 and in some instances, Group 3. The analysis of a total of 1 244 participants' (524 road show and 720 Ladies' Clubs) answers is presented in the following.

3.1   Participants' understanding of inheritance practices and the Laws of Inheritance

When exploring the general understanding of inheritance, inheritance laws and the making of a will, the following trends can be observed.

128

341 road show participants of Group 1, 146 Ladies' Clubs' participants of Group 2 and 78 participants of Group 3 stated that the distribution of the property of the deceased
- causes the suffering of the wife and the children,
- causes hatred between immediate and extended family members,
- causes *ngozi*,
- is a crime.

Respondents described their understanding of inheritance as a disadvantage a married woman faces with regard to property. In case of the death of the spouse, women would be left with nothing. Participants also pointed out that although a woman had the choice to refuse widow inheritance, she would then have to return to her natal family and leave her children behind. 152 men and 203 women of Group 1, 214 women of Group 2 and 282 women of Group 3 shared this view. As one participant from Group 2 puts it,

> "The viewers at first did not understand about the laws of inheritance and the writing of wills before viewing the feature. They were saying that when the husband dies, the wife should go back to her parents' home and they would take all the property and tell her to go back to her home because what she had come here for is no more" (excerpt from a Group 2 questionnaire).

The fact that this understanding resembled Group 3 members' answers, might point to the fact that the understanding was based on a common practice that disadvantages women.

3.2 Change as a result of watching the film

Did participants experience a change as a result of watching *Neria* (or participating in the inheritance programme respectively) and if so, how did they describe it? Looking at Group 2 and Group 3 results, 24 percent of Group 2 participants changed by stating their intention to write a will, while 11 percent of each group saw that the property should belong to the immediate family and the household goods should be registered in the woman's name. Another 10 percent changed to see that a couple should discuss all issues with each other and nine percent changed to understand that widow inheritance was no longer relevant. 56 percent of Group 3 par-

129

ticipants felt a clear increase of knowledge of the Laws of Inheritance, 11 percent saw that women must know their rights, 12 percent had experienced no change at all and nine percent felt the need to write a will.

Looking at Group 1's responses, all but four participants noted that they had experienced a change. Looking at women and men's results separately, it becomes clear that for 31 percent of the women and 54 percent of the men, this change referred to the practice of writing a will. This was followed by a change to a knowledge increase about the Laws of Inheritance and property grabbing reported by 14 percent of the women, while 16 percent of the men changed to see that the immediate, instead of the extended, family should receive all the property.

"If someone passes away, I will have pain and mourn – when my husband passed away, it took only three days for the people to collect the property. So when I saw this film I was relieved. I was given new ideas to go to the court" (excerpt from a Group 1 woman's questionnaire).

What becomes clear is that, through watching the film, a feeling of having experienced a major change was promoted. Issues related to inheritance such as widow inheritance, the need to register items also in the woman's name and the understanding that a harmonious relationship, as portrayed in the film by Patrick and Neria, assists to avoid inheritance havoc, were triggered by the film and the discussion format, so it seems, as the answers of Group 2 appear most focused.

3.3   Understanding the film messages

Participants from Group 1 and 2 listed a number of film messages they had received (see Table 5 below). The majority of all participants (134 men and 90 women of Group 1 as well as 108 women of Group 2) felt that writing a will before getting sick was the main message of the film. While this is a clear film message, it was also one of the main messages of the inheritance session. This was followed by the idea that the widow or the widower and the children are the main beneficiaries of the property (as perceived by each 32 women and men of Group 1 and 46 women of Group 2). Other messages that were received by a majority are the understanding of how property will be distributed without a will, that one should work for the

130

immediate family only, as well as the understanding that one needs advice from friends, and work in projects, and widow inheritance cannot be forced. These are main messages of the film and were understood well. What is interesting is the similarity of messages listed by Group 1 and 2. However, Group 2 women received more messages, presumably due to an extensive discussion of the film and related issues. Looking at messages listed by themes, nine messages out of 18 messages are related to the Laws of Inheritance and formal procedures. All of these reflect an increased knowledge and/or a correct interpretation of the messages. Nine messages are related to social aspects of inheritance (customs as well as informal procedures) and reflect a changed understanding regarding oppressive customs as well as strategies to avoid problems that were observed in the film. In general, primary messages of the film were understood and rein-forced through the inheritance session and the discussion format applied by Group 2 participants.

Table 5 - Film messages listed by participants

Message	Group 1 Women (248)	Men (276)	All (524)	Group 2 (360)	TOTAL (884)
1. You should write a will before[72] you get sick	90	134	224	108	332
2. The widow/widower and the children are the beneficiaries of the property of the deceased husband/wife – even without marriage certificate	32	32	64	46	110
3. I understood how property is distributed without a will	18	26	44	23	79

---

[72] To write a will before getting sick refers to the understanding that traditionally, one only thinks of uttering one's wishes when one becomes ill and feels that death is near. The oral will, for example, was made known when a person was about to die. To write a will before getting sick therefore refers to a double change - the understanding that a will must be written down and should be planned ahead.

4. Some relatives grab what they did not work for – we should work for our families and not our relatives	16	28	44	22	66
5. You need to get advice from friends and work in projects	20	6	26	35	61
6. Widow inheritance cannot be forced – the woman can choose	16	8	24	32	56
7. When facing inheritance-related problems you must report the case	16	8	24	19	43
8. After the death of a partner you should not sit, but continue to work hard to keep the family	12	8	20	15	35
9. Property distribution without law is a crime	12	6	18	17	35
10. Greed and cruelty destroys family relations	10	12	22	0	22
11. Without a will a lawyer can sort out your problems	0	0	0	13	13
12. When mourning you need to watch out for property grabbing	0	0	0	11	11
13. The culture should be amended with a change in life style	0	8	8	0	8
14. A marriage should be registered	0	0	0	8	8
15. We should follow our culture	6	0	0	0	6
16. The woman's name should occur on all important papers (title deeds, bank book, etc.)	0	0	0	5	5
17. Without will there can be problems with the property distribution	0	0	0	3	3
18. There should be discussion amongst family members	0	0	0	3	3
TOTAL	**248**	**276**	**524**	**360**	**884**

3.4 How to solve inheritance-related problems

When asked which systems for solving problems, related to widow inheritance and property grabbing, exist in participants' communities, the following systems were mentioned[73] (Graph 8 below).

Graph 8 – Ways of solving inheritance-related problems

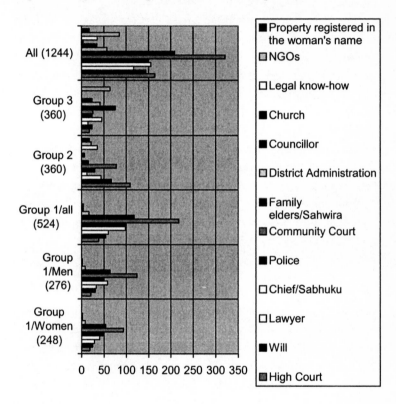

Most men of Group 1 suggested the Community Court, followed by family elders or *sahwira* (a close friend) and chiefs or *sabhuku* (a traditional leader). Women also mentioned the Community Court first, followed by family elders or *sahwira* and the police. Ladies' Clubs' participants from

---

[73] Note that people could mention more than one option.

Group 2 named the High Court first, followed by the Community Court and the will. Some participants pointed out that although they usually consulted family elders, they had now been provided with new ideas (like the will) to settle problems in a way they favoured. Others said they consulted chiefs, but suggested that traditional leaders needed training in order to understand and promote the new law, since their ways of judging were still disadvantaging women.

While Group 2 participants listed the High Court (as viewed in the film), Group 3 participants' (who had not seen the film) first choice of support systems was family elders or *sahwira*, followed by NGOs, chiefs or *sabhuku*, the High Court and knowledge about the laws. These results are in line with baseline survey findings made by K2 Techtop Consult (2001: 38) to establish knowledge, practices and awareness levels of Zimbabweans regarding inheritance-related dispute resolution. This was, however, assessed before participants had received any information about the Laws of Inheritance, while Group 3 responses were obtained after attending the inheritance session. However, Group 2's results can rather point to the fact that the extensive discussion of issues and the exposure to the film assisted in an awareness change concerning the type of support systems that can be consulted when facing inheritance-related problems.

3.5 Possible change of systems due to the film

Asked whether the film could have any influence on inheritance-related support systems as far as nature, scope or quality is concerned, Group 1's both female and male participants as well as Group 2 participants were certain about the influence. While most of the participants stated that there would definitely be an immediate felt change, some saw a change happening only with time and more teaching. As far as Group 1 is concerned, 242 women and 264 men stated that there would be a change. However, some participants gave explanations, which are listed below. Note that six women and 12 men believed there would be no change. As far as Group 2 is concerned, 320 out of 360 people believed there was a change (note that seven did not answer the question), while 193 gave reasons. As can be seen

134

in Graph 9 below, 26 percent of all participants stated that the film provided people with knowledge of their rights and knowledge of accessible support systems when being faced with inheritance-related problems (mainly Group 2 participants). 23 percent of all participants mentioned a felt change of character triggered by the viewing of the film (mainly Group 1 participants). 14 percent attributed the change to the new law, which was believed to lighten the situation for widows, and another 10 percent felt this law needed to be accepted and followed before a change could take place.

Graph 9 – Change of systems as a result of the film's impact

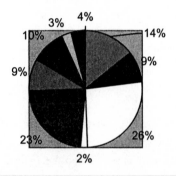

▨ The law makes it lighter for widows
■ Greed will disappear
☐ People now have knowledge of their rights/of support systems
☐ Change will come if women stand together
■ The film teaches and changes the character
▨ Change will come with time
■ People need to follow the law
☐ Change will come when people write a will
■ The oppressive tradition of giving the property to the relatives will come to an end

While Group 1 participants, for example, perceived that the oppressive tradition of allocating property to the relatives could now be ended, mainly also by writing a will, Group 2 participants felt a change needed to be facilitated by women's unity (which was not mentioned by Group 1) and which leads to the assumption that the Ladies' Clubs' set-up can support the formation/maintenance of support groups.

3.6 Questions concerning the film and the programme

The overall majority of Group 1 (364 participants) stated they had no further questions, while 92 people from Group 1 (58 men and 34 women) raised questions related to the Laws of Inheritance and 68 people (46 women and 22 men) raised questions related to the film *Neria*. Questions concerning the Laws of Inheritance reflected the need to follow up on the legal information provided - half an hour discussion and half an hour film will certainly not be enough to answer all questions concerning experienced inheritance problems. However, the questions raised by people give ideas on issues that have not yet been accepted such as benefits for second wives (which was not supported by the majority of men and even women). As far as the questions related to the film are concerned, answers reflected that people who had not previously watched the feature film were sometimes stranded when seeing the support video only. Others were confused about the new information they received. How could it be possible that the court and the elders were consulted at the same time (these two options seemed to exclude each other), or how could a widow be inherited by her child? Men seemed to be worried how their family could be supported when the widow received all the property.

In Group 2, 49 women had no answer to this question and 247 women had no further questions. 19 women asked questions related to the film and 45 women asked questions concerning the laws. Questions concerning the film cored mainly around Phineas' rude behaviour which people could not understand. Questions concerning the laws cored around the surviving spouse as main beneficiary and how to write a will.

136

Clearly more Group 1 participants raised questions, mainly concerning the Laws of Inheritance. This can be explained with the lack of follow-up after screening films to large crowds. It seems that an extensive discussion after the film enhanced the understanding of the message content. However, questions concerning the laws can furthermore point to the fact that the laws are quite complicated and can hardly be fully understood even after a comprehensive unit (such as Group 2's programme). There is a clear need for a further follow-up on messages and the simultaneous use of other media to ensure people are knowledgeable about the laws and are in a position to correctly apply the laws when they are faced with problems.

3.7 Participants' view on the media used

Out of 874 participants who had answered the question, a total of 489 out of 521 participants from Group 1 stated a preference for video, while 415 (200 women and 215 men) gave different reasons for this preference. 286 out of 353 Group 2 participants said they favoured video, while 251 gave reasons for this (see Graph 10 below).

However, there was considerable difference between Shona and Ndebele viewers. While Shona viewers felt the film aroused emotions which helped them to understand the issues, the majority of Ndebele viewers felt that, with a film, you could see for yourself and learn at the same time. To view examples of everyday experiences was felt to be powerful, especially by men of Group 1. Video was furthermore perceived to be the better medium in the face of limited educational and communicative infrastructure. Only Group 2 participants mentioned that with film, one could learn better as a group. However, not all participants believed video could stand on its own to bring across messages effectively (32 people from Group 1 - 11 women and 21 men - and 67 people from Group 2). They suggested the film should be accompanied by pamphlets, and the information needed to be channelled through additional sources such as radio and discussions.

Graph 10 – Participants' view on the media used

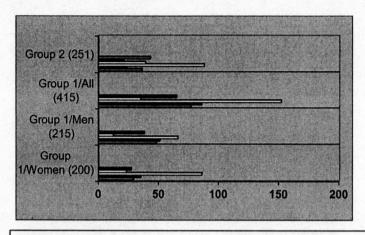

- ▨ We prefer film because we can see and learn as a group
- ■ Film is best because not everyone can read or has a radio
- ☐ The film arouses emotions which changes minds
- ☐ The film allows you to see for yourself and learn at the same time
- ■ The film shows us examples of our everyday experiences
- ▨ The film is most appropriate to transfer messages

3.8 Lessons derived from the film

As listed in Graph 11 below[74], the majority of Group 1 and 2 members derived that they should write a will before getting sick. Further, men from Group 1 felt they learnt to respect the law when distributing property and to condemn greedy behaviour. Women from Group 1 mainly learnt the lesson that the law could assist even without a marriage certificate, to respect the law when distributing the property and to work hard when the spouse has

---

[74] Note that more than one answer was possible.

passed away. Group 2 participants understood that widow inheritance can not be forced, to accept advice from friends and to work hard when the partner has passed away.

Graph 11 – Lessons derived from the film

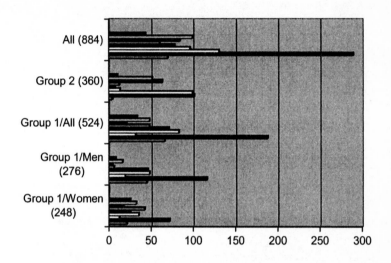

■ To know that spouses are the rightful beneficiaries

☐ To work hard when your partner has passed away

■ To accept advice from friends

▨ To understand that one can benefit even when married customarily

■ To condemn greed because it destroys family relations

☐ To respect the law when distributing the property

☐ To understand that widow inheritance cannot be forced

■ To write a will before getting sick

▨ To learn about the law and wills

Group 2 participants' answers were much more focused and their lessons reflect clear empowerment skills such as the need to exchange ideas with others, the need to be economically self-reliant and to refuse oppressive customs through action. While the majority of all participants clearly felt that a will needs to be written in the future, it appears that a combination of the *Neria* material and an extensive discussion about the film can heighten the learning effects of participants.

3.9 Will there be a change for widows and widowers?

Asked if lessons derived will influence the situation for widows and widowers, the following trend can be stated.

The firm belief that it is going to change or has changed already was stated by all but one participant from Group 1 (523) and Group 2 (360). Reasons given for a belief in change are similar in both groups:

1. Increased knowledge about laws will allow people (women in particular, but also men and children) to exercise their rights, reduce the incidents of property grabbing in particular and ill-treatment of widows in general.

2. The film in particular raises awareness and is a medium that initiates change.

3. Behavioural change (e.g. the writing of wills; being faithful) triggered by the programme will make life easier for everyone.

4. The new law is fair and will replace a custom that was not fair (unfair property distribution, widow inheritance).

5. The new law will make sure that the property will be left for those who worked for it (Group 2 participants only).

"Yes, it will change and we should tell our husbands that we make a will together before we die. Then we sort the life for those remaining behind" (excerpt from a Group 2 questionnaire).

"It will change because women and men know their rights and know where to go when they need help" (excerpt from a Group 2 questionnaire).

"Those who saw the film long back have already changed their mind about those whose husbands or wives passed away because the person will be knowing what to do. Others without deceased husbands or wives will marry according to 5.11 and write the wills and keep them at the bank or church" (excerpt from a Group 2 questionnaire).

3.10 Other comments

Given an additional opportunity to air their views, the following categories of answers given by participants can be differentiated. Group 1 participants' suggestions can be divided into the following categories:

- Request to show the whole film of *Neria*,
- Request to show other films on issues of importance such as HIV/AIDS,
- Request to visit the rural areas (and rural schools in particular) more frequently, especially with the road shows,
- Request to increase promotion activities before screening a film (posters, announcements),
- Request to provide the communities with written material/promotion material to enforce the impact of the film.

Group 2 participants contributed the following ideas:

- Request to repeat the programme at the workplace of husbands or during church meetings,
- Request to repeat the programme at various leisure venues such as beer-halls and cinemas,
- Request to show more films, especially those on how to make a will,
- Request to provide free legal aid.

4 Feedback from the road show and Ladies' Clubs' report

The report provided by Experiential Momentum in December 2002 at the end of the Wills and Inheritance Laws Programme suggests similar findings to those described above. According to this report, most people at road shows commented that more time needed to be spent on the subject and more booklets needed to be made available to people, so that they are empowered to discuss such issues with their families as they affect them. As Experiential Momentum put it,

"It should however be mentioned that the message has reached/touched many people, some of whom have confessed to be in similar situations and others who want to learn more in case they find themselves in that situation" (2002: 4).

As far as Ladies' Clubs are concerned, Experiential Momentum demonstrators reported that the women found the sessions very informative as they admitted not knowing much about wills and inheritance laws. Other women who were aware of the laws asked whether they could invite their husbands to these sessions or whether they could be visited at their workplaces. Most of them said they were afraid to bring up the subject with their husbands, as the general (Shona) belief is that husbands mysteriously die when they write wills (Experiential Momentum 2002).

Another reason for the need of husbands to attend the sessions was to hear what they have to say for themselves as far as the new laws are concerned. The amendment, so some women felt, promoted prostitution and polygamy and allowed second wives to reap where they did not sow (Experiential Momentum 2002). In general, comments from the women were positive and encouraging. These included statements about how participants benefited through increased knowledge and awareness, and statements about the writing of a will to avoid inheritance-related problems.

"The session on wills brought new vision and wisdom to my life. I feel challenged to discuss inheritance laws with my husband" (Experiential Momentum 2002: 3).

Chapter VI
Ways of thinking, feeling and behaving -
the potential of video in education for empowerment

1 The empowerment potential of *Neria* from a communication theory perspective

This study aimed at exploring attitudinal change triggered by the observation of characters in a film and by being exposed to persuasive messages. As the discussion in Chapter I suggests, it is important that favourable cognitive responses are evoked through messages that relate to existing knowledge, values and interests of target groups. What transpired from participants' remarks is that credibility of the characters, similarity of characters' experiences to those of participants, and authority of the characters to promote the new behaviour, were important criteria in the process of attitude change. The fact that Group 2's answers seemed, however, much more focused, was explained with the different learning environment.

According to *Social Cognitive Theory*, para-social interaction, prompt role modelling, efficacy and the creation of a social learning environment are key elements in attitude change through observation. The concepts will be observed in more detail below.

1.1 Para-social interaction

Most of the perceived changes of participants can be attributed to the film's interactivity patterns, which can be found throughout the film. Para-social interaction occurred on three levels - cognition, affect and behaviour or behavioural intention. The first refers to thoughtful para-social interaction (the process of thinking about the characters' actions). People discovered the relevance of the film's message to their lives and the need to interact. The second deals with emotional para-social interaction (the process of identifying with a particular media character and believing that her or his interests are linked). Emotional involvement with the lives of the characters

143

stimulated learning from characters' experiences. The third refers to behavioural interaction (the overt reaction to characters) mainly reflected in talking about the characters and issues of their concern.

1.2 Prompt role modelling

As far as modelling is concerned the entertainment education programme promoted the social desirability (the planning for the future by writing a will, for example, or the advantage of pursuing one's rights), or undesirability (property grabbing, for example) of certain behaviours as enacted by appealing characters (like Neria or Patrick) or unappealing characters (like Phineas or Maria). Participants were provided with behavioural examples. Interactivity patterns discussed above were important to trigger aspects of modelling as well as the stage of reproduction (in the process of attitude and behavioural change). The viewer was allowed to practise a new behaviour through the characters, in a safe and non-threatening environment. Aspects of modelling further occurred when the role models stimulated and promoted social learning and behaviour. The character of Neria, for example, was believable, familiar to the viewers, and triggered an emotional reaction in viewers. Most of the people stated that they felt sorry about what had happened to Neria. This led to a situation where people felt receptive to the message, the strategy, or the solution to either avoid hassles, or to take up action to get back what is rightfully theirs.

1.3 Efficacy

Self-efficacy (the belief in one's ability to organise action in order to manage different situations) could clearly be shown to have developed. Furthermore, collective efficacy, according to which people have the confidence in joint capabilities, to fulfil set goals, and to face opposition (as listed here under the emotional empowerment component), was increased, too. This is crucial as in order to achieve change, people need to believe that they can solve their mutually experienced problems through unified effort. The characters were found to have effectively stimulated and promoted social learning because they were believable, they expressed emotions, they were attractive and resembled the viewers. As perceived experts, they promoted desirable behaviour and were accepted.

1.4   The social learning environment

As a result of the modelling, audience members could talk to one another about a number of issues. This resulted in the creation of a social learning environment in which new ideas could be tested. As was pointed out in Chapter I, these tests must include the judging of the new behaviour against criteria such as compatibility or complexity. The promoted behaviour of

- Writing a will before getting sick,
- Enforcing the right of choice to remarry after being widowed,
- Enforcing the right of the immediate family as main beneficiaries,
- Accepting advice from friends and working in projects,
- Reporting inheritance-related abuse,

was discussed thoroughly and was said to be discussed with others who could not attend that specific session. This is important as the discussion of new behaviour within social learning environments, of 'empowerment peer groups', facilitates the spread of a new behaviour and can, through constant and thorough discussion, develop into a new social norm. Moreover, it could be shown that messages are stronger when discussed in groups, after seeing the film, as reflected in the results of road show participants as opposed to Ladies' Clubs' viewers, or focus group discussions.

1.5   Behavioural change

When behaviour is being tested in the above-mentioned social learning environments, behaviour change can be sparked. At this stage, mainly people with a very high degree of intention will be performing the behaviour. However, one needs to bear in mind that practising behaviour once does not automatically mean it will be practised continually. Research has shown that people who perform behaviour at irregular intervals may have experienced unpleasant consequences or barriers, and may, therefore, require support or reinforcement for their behaviour. Only then can they become advocates of the new behaviour (see Chapter I; point 2.4).

As a result, people might convert behavioural intentions mentioned above into behaviour and might demand more and better information, not only on the subject of inheritance and the law, but also on other issues of their concern. This will help to understand all kinds of information, which might in the long run affect knowledge, awareness and interest (emotional and cognitive components respectively). The more people discuss the new behaviour, the more likely it will be that abuse is being reported. The more it is reported, the greater will be the awareness in the communities and the easier it will be for affected parties to make their voices heard.

2   *Neria*'s empowerment potential - the measurement framework

As was mentioned in Chapter I, empowerment can be measured through the various components addressed by a specific programme. The changes it brings in terms of women's individual understanding and collective action, strength and stability of the support group where learning takes place, or objectives identified for future action are some of the indicators of this change. When applying the empowerment framework in order to measure the impact of *Neria* on audiences (Chapter I; point 3), each empowerment component needs to be regarded separately in order to observe if a change has taken place. This will be done below.

2.1   The cognitive component

Once relevant skills are transmitted, cognitive changes such as awareness and knowledge increase (in this case, especially on the Laws of Inheritance), an understanding of the self and the ability to name problems and to identify solutions should be felt. If changed beliefs or opinions were expressed with regard to these indicators will be explored below.

146

2.1.1 Understanding the self and the need to make choices that might be against cultural and social expectations

Whilst discussing the change experienced through watching the film, the understanding that widow inheritance is not compulsory (gained by Group 1 and 2), that the immediate family should receive the property (as perceived by men of Group 1 and Group 2 members) as well as the need to work for the immediate instead of the extended family (men of Group 1 and members of Group 2) reflect the understanding for a need to make choices against cultural and social expectations.

2.1.2 Acquiring new knowledge especially about legal rights

This refers mainly to the understanding that women and children are rightful beneficiaries of property (mainly mentioned by Group 2). That the will can be a remedy, and property distribution without law is a crime (as understood by Group 1 men and members of Group 2), are further examples of a knowledge increase. It reflects particularly in the category 'change through the film', where the new knowledge refers to the Laws of Inheritance and how to report property grabbing (Group 3, Group 2, women of Group 1), the understanding that the law can assist even without a marriage certificate (Group 1 women, Group 2), that household goods should be registered in the woman's name (Group 2), the knowledge of where to get help (Group 2 and Group 3) as well as learning about the law and wills (Group 1 men). Participants learnt to consider the High Court (Group 2), the will (Group 2, Group 1), and the lawyer (Group 1, Group 2) as new aid possibilities.

It reflects, further, in participants' recommendations; particularly in the request for additional information on inheritance or HIV/AIDS issues (Group 1). Many participants stated that the film changed them into persons, who are more aware of legal rights and more sensitised to rights violation, which happens in their neighbourhoods or in their own families. The intentions this new awareness can trigger are described below.

2.1.3 Ability to name problems and to identify action leading to solutions

The ability to identify action leading to solutions was increased, mainly, through understanding film messages or messages gained from the film. The following action was proposed:

a) To write a will before getting sick (Group 1 men, Group 2),

b) To respect the law when distributing the property (Group 1 men),

c) To condemn greed since it destroys family relations (Group 1 men),

d) To discuss all issues with each other as husband and wife (Group 1 women, Group 2),

e) To get advice from friends and work in projects (Group 2, Group 1 women),

f) To report one's case (Group 2, Group 1 women),

g) To continue to work hard after being widowed (Group 2, Group 1 women),

h) To register one's marriage (Group 2).

All groups who have watched the film gained a clear understanding that property distribution without a will, or without the Laws of Inheritance, can be problematic. Problems that might occur when neglecting the laws were listed and action to counter these problems were mentioned. While some of the action reflects behaviour that was promoted in the film (such as a), b) d) e), f) and g), others are rather a result of an analysis of the promoted behaviour such as c) or h).

2.1.4 Limitations

Communication barriers[75] are inevitable and constitute limitations within the cognitive empowerment process. As questions related to the film re-

---

[75] Barriers, which hinder the growth of communication, are usually erected when the sender or the receiver of a message has problems adjusting to the interaction partner. Reasons why they occur can be: the use of complicated language, the non-incorporation of participants' ideas, unclear messages, a climate of non-trust and insecurity, message reception but no comprehension, mental turbulence, misunderstanding or biased listen-

vealed, the new information about the possibility of combining state law and traditional law resulted rather in confusion for some Group 1 women and, to some extent, some Group 2 members. Also, the portrayed choice of widow inheritance (by giving the traditional items to the child) led, in a number of cases, to perplexity. Questions related to the Laws of Inheritance, furthermore, revealed that not everyone seemed to have received all the necessary details on how to write a will or on certain procedures of property distribution according to state laws, which resulted in confusion amongst, especially, Group 1 men. A feeling of anger, which was, for example, generated by the information that second wives in polygynous situations have to receive a share from the deceased's estate, resulted in building up resistance, especially amongst Group 1 men. This form of message reception with limited comprehension needs to be taken seriously, since it can, as outlined above, create serious barriers to attitude and behaviour change and to a cognitive empowerment process.

2.2 The emotional component

Emotional empowerment can take place when emotion is evoked, a feeling of self-confidence is developed and a belief that one can succeed in one's efforts is formed. As a result, changed feelings and beliefs should be expressed.

2.2.1 Emotion evoked

That emotion was evoked during the viewing of the film can be seen in a number of statements made by different group members. Especially the 'suffering' of the widow was felt to be heart-rending and touched people's feelings. Particularly women from Group 1 and Group 2 members stated that they had experienced a personal change through seeing an innocent person suffering and finally experiencing justice. Participants' view on the media revealed a similar feeling: film, they felt, aroused emotions, which

---

ing. Distraction due to noise, as it occurs in large crowds, is another crucial reason for barriers to occur.

changed minds (Group 2, Group 1 women). Other comments suggested that participants, who had personally experienced inheritance-related problems, got so involved emotionally that they started to cry when *Neria* cried. Participants mentioned that they felt as if they were going through their problems again, but were this time supplied with options for action, which made them feel 'good and strong'.

2.2.2 Development of a feeling of self-confidence

Statements clearly revealed that this feeling could particularly be developed amongst Group 2 members. Often, it was mentioned that people now felt equipped with information or skills to counter problems. People felt stronger to discuss taboo issues with family members such as their spouses. Women further pointed out that they were now certain not to endure oppressive tradition or practices, since they have learnt that there was a choice. A 'new self-confidence' was reported. Members of Group 1 also voiced their firm belief in a positive change for widows in general and a confidence in actively contributing towards this change.

2.2.3 The formation of a belief that one can succeed in one's efforts

The firm belief in change is a clear indicator for the belief that one can actually succeed if one is equipped with necessary skills. The feeling that a change will come as long as women stand together in this issue reflects this, too (Group 2). It was felt that especially increased legal knowledge will allow people (women in particular, but also men and children) to exercise their rights and will reduce the incidents of property grabbing, in particular, and ill-treatment of widows, in general (Group 2, Group 1). A trust in the behavioural change of others (such as the writing of wills and being faithful) could further be built up. Group 2 as well as Group 1 members strongly believed that greed would disappear and there would be peace as a result of watching the film.

2.2.4 Limitations

As discussed under 2.1.4 above, communication barriers will also have effects on the emotional component. The fact that widow inheritance as a choice (as opposed to a must) confused a number of women might in fact hinder the development of a feeling that a woman can make a choice against 'oppressive practices', as they were frequently called by women.

2.3 The political component

By facilitating reflective spaces for individuals who share certain disadvantages, political empowerment can take place. As they group together in order to discuss experiences and formulate strategies to counter their disadvantaged situations, their voices can be made heard with an impact on their environment. An individual awareness, collective action as well as the intention to apply the promoted behaviour should be felt.

2.3.1 Ability to analyse the environment in political and social terms (individual awareness)

This ability, so it is believed, reflects clearly and overlaps with findings made under 2.1.3 (such as the ability to identify action leading to solutions). It requires analytical skills to understand the world around one, to realise the structures of a problem and to see the need of solving it. This awareness, as has been shown throughout the study, could be raised. It includes recognition of unnecessary oppression of women through certain inheritance practices and the restriction of women to choose what they really want (without being threatened, for example, that their children will be taken away or other cruel sanctions will be implemented). It extends further to a sense of ownership of assets one has contributed to.

2.3.2 Ability to organise and mobilise for social change (collective action) and the participation in non-family groups

There was a felt need to extend the programme and its information to others. While this referred mainly to rural women, who were reported to be more disadvantaged than their urban counterparts, Group 2 members suggested strategies to extend the information to men, in general, by repeating the programme at strategic venues of men such as beer-halls. This was felt to be of extreme importance in order to ensure a simultaneous learning process of men as well as enabling them to carry out frank discussions with their wives, mothers, girl-friends or daughters.

It was emphasised that learning needs a group in order to discuss and take action. People clearly felt encouraged to participate also in non-family groups. The intended participation in income-generating projects where one has the opportunity to discuss and share knowledge reflects this. Information on how to form new support groups was requested mainly by Group 1 women, but, also, Group 2 members (who belonged to already established customer clubs), expressed their wish to form groups or participate in non-family groups, which, so they believed, could provide them with comfort, support and trustworthy advice.

2.3.3 Intention to apply the new, promoted behaviour

In summary, the following intentions to implement the new behaviour were stated:
- Intention to write a will (Group 1 men, Group 2),
- Intention to accept advice from friends and work in projects (Group 2, Group 1 women),
- Intention to respect the law when distributing the property (Group 1 men),
- Intention to report a case to the authorities (Group 2, Group 1 women),
- Intention to be more alert during the mourning period (Group 2),
- Intention to work hard when the partner has passed away (Group 2, Group 1 women),

152

- Intention to look for further information on the Laws of Inheritance (Group 1),
- Intention to act against the extended family when discovering greedy behaviour (Group 1 men).

As has been discussed earlier, these intentions are strong indicators for a future behavioural change. However, external factors can influence the decision if the behaviour is actually implemented and sustained. They will be discussed below (2.6).

2.3.4 Support of disadvantaged groups in giving their perspective

Disadvantaged groups, such as widows, have clearly been supported in verbalising their perspective through the programme. Whereas before, inheritance-related issues such as property grabbing or widow inheritance were still difficult to address, people constantly came forward and explained that they were empowered to talk about these issues in public. Most of the female programme participants stated that although they were given a tool to address these issues, they could not do so effectively in women-only groups. Only a rather small number of, especially, Group 2 members said they now felt free to discuss taboo issues with their husbands at home. They made suggestions to utilise the tool in men-only groups, too, or to show the film and discuss related issues in mixed groups. However, here, clearly the learning environment, in which the film has been used, reflects positive empowering aspects for those who have discussed these issues thoroughly. This does not only become clear when looking at Group 2's responses compared to Group 1's but also as one recalls the preliminary study's results summarised in Chapter III (2.4f) or results from focus group discussions during the material development exercise highlighted in Chapter IV (2.2.3f).

Widows, who were facing disadvantages through a number of different constraints, were given a voice through the film *Neria*. Widows, who were, at that point in time, condemned to struggle without much notice, were clearly empowered to discuss their issues at different levels of society. However, as comments suggest, widowers, who face problems similar to widows have not been supported in a satisfactory manner. Although the message of the film, as well as of the inheritance session, emphasised that *spouses* should be beneficiaries of the property of the deceased, it seems that the female example in the film, as well as the focus on the female support group, has not facilitated a positive attitude change towards men who have lost their partners. Although this issue has been specifically dealt with in the *Neria* support manual, it needs a much stronger emphasis when the material is utilised.

It should not be forgotten that it is as much taboo to talk about women's issues outside the family as it is culturally unacceptable for a man to admit his inability to deal with a certain situation, his lack of knowledge as well as his emotional problems caused by the death of his partner. Issues, like property grabbing, psychological manipulation, or the removal of children from the remaining father's home against his wish need to be discussed just as much in public, since this behaviour and practice stem from the same negative attitudes within society.

2.4   The economic component

To see the need to engage in income-generation for economic autonomy was clearly stimulated by the viewing of the film. A number of women stated that they needed to work hard after their partner has passed away in order to earn a living. They mentioned that one should not sit on one's hands and wait for others to supply, but it was felt to be crucial to have one's own income to provide for the family. Others suggested that one's own income would make one more independent in her or his choices after a partner had passed away. However, a number of women, especially from Group 2, realised the need to register all household property (all property that was acquired together in a marriage) in the woman's name, in order not to be stranded financially when inheritance-related problems came up. A separate bank account where proceeds from independent activities are kept, was moreover perceived to heighten economic autonomy and was clearly triggered through the film's example, where the widow was completely dependent on her in-laws because they had stolen the bank book with joint savings that were unfortunately registered in the husband's name only.

2.5 Attitude change and behavioural intention

Attitudes shaped by culture, such as the idea that women need to give in to traditional practices (like widow inheritance), could be changed, through seeing a positive example of a woman who managed to stand up and succeed against the extended family. A large number of female participants felt they should discuss all issues with their husbands (like the film couple's example) and learnt to see that this behaviour can be helpful for the climate at home. Discussions in the house, so it was suggested, should extend to issues of relevance for both partners, which include discussion about death and its consequences for remaining family members.

Other changes mentioned were the understanding that wills should be written down, that they should be written also by women, and that they should be written and discussed together with their husbands. Another cultural issue such as the property distribution, in favour of the husband's relatives, could be addressed by making people aware that this practice leads to the suffering, not only of the remaining partner, but also of the deceased's children.

While participants felt that a change could only be achieved by some form of action (personal or group), many women saw a change enabled mainly by external support groups, such as NGOs or the government that - so women believed or uttered - would enforce the law's implementation through proactive court or police officers. That this belief does also point to constraints and can actually hinder empowerment will be explored below.

2.6 The enabling environment

What other criteria are important to facilitate a change of attitude and behaviour? In many cases the environment by which individuals and groups are surrounded, can play a crucial role to either support or discourage newly learnt skills, attitude change or new behaviour. External factors will certainly be decisive if or if not the behaviour will be reinforced and advocated and if it can finally become a norm. Frankly, it would be naive to assume that one screening of *Neria*, the use of the support video or the manual, could persuade participants to a sustainable behavioural change.

Although it could be shown that awareness of certain issues was raised and current attitudes and practices were partially revised, the environment in which the participants live clearly poses severe constraints to a sustainable change. The following points should highlight these constraints and suggest different strategies to create or support an enabling environment that can strengthen change of behaviour and practices.

2.6.1 Follow-up programmes

It has been mentioned very often that this type of programme should be repeated frequently to allow for a follow-up of a particular exercise. However, constraints that have been encountered while implementing this programme can reveal why follow-up programmes might not be implemented in the near future or might need to consider long implementation periods and high resource input. The implementation of educational activities is generally hindered by an inability of group participants to reach the screening destinations due to economic hardships. In times of severe economic crisis priorities of participants do change. While it is certainly extremely necessary to know how to apply the Laws of Inheritance and to know how one can exercise one's rights, this might become unimportant in the face of starvation and the simple struggle for survival on a daily basis. People might simply not have the time to attend a programme, unless food or transport is provided.

2.6.2 Support structures for disadvantaged community members

Whenever people saw the film, the issue of support structures was discussed extensively. It was frequently mentioned that *Neria* stresses the importance of formal support structures (such as the courts or lawyers) only. However, in remote areas, there are no state courts and no lawyers and so the use of the law becomes therefore a problem for those who do not live in reach of support services. Even if courts are in an acceptable reach of people, experience shows that court processes are so bureaucratic that it can take years for decisions to be made and effects to be accomplished. To register an estate and to go through all necessary procedures will depend on different agents who are themselves overworked, are part of an ineffective environment, or are sometimes not capable and knowledgeable enough to handle the various cases. The high death rate (mainly due to the HIV/AIDS pandemic) and the rapidly increasing number of inheritance cases that need to be dealt with, worsen the situation. Capacities, it seems, are simply not coping with this immense task. People who have been made to believe that the support services are simply 'waiting for them' end up feeling lost and helpless and sometimes lack the energy to continuously follow-up on their cases.

2.6.3 Advocacy of new behaviour

How can new behaviour be advocated in the face of social and cultural constraints? It was found that many problems originate from negative cultural and social attitudes. Expectations of class, position, age and gender can play an important role in facilitating and supporting change of practices - or hindering it. While it is certainly crucial that women are empowered to see their disadvantaged situation and to implement strategies to counter these disadvantages, especially at community level, it will still be in the hands of established decision-makers in how far these strategies can be implemented and with what effect. Therefore, there is a clear need to accept local decision-makers (especially in absence of other support systems such as courts) such as chiefs, headmen, *sabhuku* or traditional healers and to engage in meaningful discussion about viable solutions for disadvantaged community members. They have to be continuously provided with information about the Laws of Inheritance, in a manner that is sensitive and culturally acceptable. Although a number of distributors of *Neria* material have reported that traditionalists and local leaders who had been called to watch the film, started to open up and discuss about disadvantaging practices, this will certainly not always be the case, and needs to, therefore, be systematically addressed.

What also needs to be discussed is what happens to community members who have successfully stood up against their spouse's relatives and who want to continue to live in their community. What is hardly ever mentioned is how the different parties can peacefully continue with their lives in the presence of each other. What will happen if this cannot be achieved? There must be some kind of support system that will assist those who are no longer accepted in their communities. Comments from participants suggest that the non-existence of such support or strategies will mainly hinder women to exercise their rights because they will have no place to go once they have fought their relatives in one way or another.

2.7 The potential - learning through shared experience

In general, it could be shown that the film, *Neria*, bears enormous potential in the field of perception and action change, mainly because

- it initiates in-depth discussions about the actual treatment of women in a disadvantaged legal situation especially amongst the so-called traditionalists,
- it brings women together not only to discuss similar experiences, and to get help co-operatively but also to initiate solution options on their own,
- it assists men to reassess attitudes that pose a barrier to the improvement of women's status, to initiate discussion with members of the extended family and to act in a manner that supports the advancement of women,
- it points out the difficult legal situation and the problematic transition from so-called tradition to modernity.

It was shown that the learning process aimed at triggering empowerment needs to be close to an adult's experience and should build upon the intellectual, emotional and cultural resources of learning participants. In reflective learning spaces, new ideas could be discussed amongst those who felt they share a common problem. This was clearly demonstrated by Group 2's responses compared with Group 1 or Group 3's answers, which reflected the need for a forum to discuss the film and its material thoroughly. Within the large crowd, neighbours and friends who came together to follow the programme could be seen starting to discuss on certain issues, but a thorough discussion, in most cases, did not happen.

Whilst watching the film example, people were reminded of how they have dealt with a similar situation, or they were triggered to ask themselves how they would handle this situation if they were affected. Learning could occur when a solution offered by a certain character was perceived to be realistic and portrayed as effective or more effective than the solution or strategy one had applied or intended to apply beforehand. Moreover, participants could gain confidence when sharing experiences with others. In the group, reactions of other viewers towards the promoted attitude and behaviour could be easily, which assisted in making choices. Findings of this study clearly established that participants' consciousness could be raised through the critical analysis of one's own condition, triggered by characters of an entertaining and educating film.

Positive changes resulting from this consciousness can occur at different levels, mainly at household level, at community level and at a societal level. At a family level, it might be easier for women - being equipped with a sense of personal power - to discuss inheritance-related taboo issues. To negotiate for the registration of property also in the woman's name and to write wills can be part of that process. Empowerment peer group formations can be supported at a community level, which can also assist in influencing changes at a societal level. Here, decision-makers can be sensitised to prioritise inheritance issues and can vote for the elimination of laws that discriminate against women and children, can support women in leadership and decision-making, can facilitate increased access to education for women and girls and increased access to and control over economic resources for, particularly, women.

3   Recommendations

A number of recommendations can be made for the use of video in adult education for empowerment in general, as well as for its specific use in nonformal legal education. Most of them reflect recommendations made by participants of this study. They can be divided into three categories: related to the programme format and content, related to the infrastructure concerning state law and related to informal support groups.

3.1 Programmes that effectively reach target groups

Throughout the past four years participants of different groups voiced the need for more holistic programmes that can benefit the most disadvantaged. This finding is in line with international suggestions for integrated behavioural change programmes, whereby different stakeholders participate in the programme and contribute their differences to make it work (see Rimon 2002).

3.1.1 Location and medium of transmission

Film or video has been shown to be a favoured medium in information dissemination. What became clear is the strong need for this information to be in vernacular languages. In order to transmit information that is complicated, there needs to be additional material such as books or brochures in vernacular languages in sufficient quantity to ensure that most communities are in possession of this material. Posters were also felt to assist in announcing the programme or the material's availability especially in remote areas. Then, the programme should be accompanied by regular radio lessons in vernacular languages to facilitate a thorough follow-up and to allow for wider participation of disadvantaged groups.

The feeling that one should have access to this kind of information as early in life as possible, was a reason for suggesting to target, especially, schools. It was moreover felt that through the pupils, their respective families, especially in rural areas, could also be informed about the laws and issues that core around inheritance. Then, the various churches were felt to play a crucial role in offering inheritance-related support, and gatherings were mentioned to be occasions of great importance in order to disseminate information and raise awareness on the Laws of Inheritance.

3.1.2 Group composition

It was found that so-called message films find their effective application in two ways. Mobile film units/road shows, which can bring the message to a large crowd, thereby reaching those who do not have other means of communication such as radio, television or newspapers, were the most favoured option to receive these films. The other option was to receive information through small groups. While the road show set-up with a short information session and an extensive quiz with prizes were felt to be a good introduction to the film, the follow-up after the film was felt to be ineffective. Since people were directly involved and most of them had faced similar problems before, there was a strong need for further information and clarification of issues brought up by film and information session. The fact that some people were provided with addresses of support groups in their areas, assisted but was felt to be not enough. A user-friendly discussion forum with trained counsellors after each programme is therefore highly recommended. Additionally, during a show, suggestion boxes could be put up to encourage comments and questions that could be dealt with by paralegals or support groups in the respective areas of screening. Regular meetings could be held to discuss these questions and suggestions in communities.

Small groups, on the other hand, had the advantage of using the supporting material and discussing different issues thoroughly, but could then only reach a small number of people at the same time.

Also, the group composition was frequently discussed. It was felt that women-only groups had an advantage in providing a forum for discussing similar experiences amongst women, but posed constraints in that men could not hear the discussion or share the points. It was felt that, especially, men needed to receive this information in order to facilitate a change of behaviour. Women, so it was stated, would still face enormous problems if men did not see the necessity to write wills. Mixed groups can therefore be strongly recommended even when taboo issues are discussed. It will be enormously problematic to address these issues alone at home, while in a mixed group, views can be discussed and exchanged naturally. Once taboo issues have been discussed outside the home, it can help to raise these and other issues in private also. In order to reach as many people as possible while maintaining the quality of learning, huge screenings could be combined with discussion groups that could be held after the show or, alternatively, the next day.

3.1.3 Using video in combination with supportive material

The participants' views on the choice of medium to transmit information, and their views about its influence on supporting a favourable receptivity of promoted messages, allows useful insights into the use of film/video and accompanying support material in adult education for empowerment. The statements of participants revealed clearly how film can assist this specific target group to receive messages that can lead them to change their attitudes, which might result in new behavioural intentions. Video assists in acting as an eye catcher and in helping people to visualise and recall images linked with the information intended to be transmitted. It can, moreover, stimulate attitude change when believable characters experience an attitude change during the film.

However, it must be clear that film or video can, under these specific circumstances, not stand on its own, especially when rather complicated information is being transmitted. Complex contents like inheritance laws with all their loopholes, or, for example, HIV/AIDS related information need to be transmitted in combination with written material such as books or pamphlets. It can furthermore be supported by talks (like a quiz or a lecture), preferably given by experts who can moreover answer questions after the shows. Equally important, so people stated, was the provision of details on supportive measures, or addresses of support groups after the programmes.

3.1.4 Priority for local research on entertainment that educates

What became clear is a crucial need for more careful interdisciplinary research to explore attitudes, practices and behaviour of potential beneficiaries. The incorporation of local beneficiaries into the planning, design and implementation process is a prerequisite for this task. More long-term

162

studies, that can measure effects on participants and can explore barriers to communication goals, are needed. These long-term studies need to go hand in hand with long-term programmes. To implement an initiative for a year or two is simply not enough to change behaviour widely. It should be reason for serious concern that, despite the various stakeholders, who have been active in the field for a number of years now, people at grassroots level do not seem to have benefited much. Their situation has either remained unchanged or has, sometimes, even worsened. One of the reasons for this is the relatively short programme duration that will sometimes make it impossible for all stakeholders at different levels to interact effectively. Therefore, a programme duration of a minimum of three years is strongly recommended.

3.2 Government support

The government was mentioned very often to have an obligation to contribute to an enabling environment that supports a change of behaviour and practices. Recommendations made can be found below.

3.2.1 Decentralising support structures

The fact that government institutions such as courts are simply not available in remote areas was felt to be an enormous barrier when wanting to exercise one's rights. The distances (and the resources needed to cover those distances) were reported to be too great when one wanted to register an estate or report inheritance-related abuse. Decentralisation of institutions such as courts, pension offices or the Guardian's Fund in remote areas that do not have district administration offices in their nearer reach was felt by many to be a viable solution. Paralegals employed by NGOs were also believed to represent a kind of legal authority that can, through simple personal presence or through the delivery of a formal letter to greedy relatives, for example, sometimes end discriminating behaviour towards the widow and can therefore be considered a good alternative. Paralegals could be trained in each remote community and could render advice to community members and traditional decision-makers, as an ongoing exercise.

3.2.2 Supervising support structures

Making support structures more efficient was one of the most crucial recommendations. It referred first and foremost to abusive situations created by legal personnel employed to assist people with their problems, regardless of the type of people looking for help. As far as court officials or clerks are concerned, there was a strong recommendation to organise offices in a manner that would effectively allow dealing with the rising number of support seekers. Comments referred to bigger offices, and appropriate waiting facilities but, most important, to a client-friendly atmosphere that allowed different support seekers to discuss their cases in a confidential environment. Since there are so far no alternatives to the courts in order to register estates, for example, a mentality of power over clients seems to have developed over the years, when, after all, people should be assisted in a friendly and helpful manner. Cases of bribery of court officials have been reported in alarming numbers. It is not unusual, that files disappear, which will in most cases bring the case to a halt.

If one wants to avoid dealing with the case oneself, one normally hires a lawyer, provided one has the financial means to do so. However, since most people are completely unaware of the contents of different laws and feel, at the same time, that a lawyer is an authority that cannot be questioned, lawyers have been reported to unnecessarily postpone cases, ask for high sums of money and are never available for consultation with their clients. Simple cases can so easily take up to two or three years and can be costly for the client.

Then, a large number of police officers were reported to be unhelpful when dealing with so-called domestic cases. Many incidents were recounted, where police officers either refused to deal with cases of property grabbing or domestic violence, or acted in favour of the abuser. This was mainly due to cultural attitudes or bribery.

While it is definitely necessary for people to be more confident and to question all kinds of authorities' actions, there was a strong recommendation to install a supervising body that can effectively survey processes, and take punitive action against those that are supposed to be assisting clients but are actually abusing them. If this is not available, it is impossible to go further than awareness raising with any given programme, since behaviour and practices just cannot be changed when the institutions that carry out the necessary procedures are perpetuating the abuse.

3.2.3 Enforcing the Laws of Inheritance

A large number of people felt that the government should prioritise the issue of inheritance. In order to discourage lawbreakers such as property grabbers, people felt there should be harsh sentences for those who abused the law and this information should be published, in order to have a model character. Hard labour was, for example, one of the suggested punishments. In general, people felt that there was much more positive publicity needed on the benefits of the Laws of Inheritance and the necessity to prioritise the immediate family as beneficiaries of the estate. This publicity should come preferably from people who are considered to be authorities or leaders.

3.2.4 Allocating resources

Almost all participants mentioned that the costs involved in applying the Laws of Inheritance posed serious constraints. Fees for a court messenger, publishing information regarding the estate, or other payments necessary in the process, were felt to be unaffordable by many. To offer free legal aid for those who are not employed was a strong recommendation. Although the Ministry of Justice has opened the Legal Aid Directorate to assist those clients, (which is a very effective example of how some court officials, pensions' officers or lawyers could assist their clientele), one office is simply not enough to cope with the growing number of cases. While more resources (not only monetary but also human) should be allocated to this sector, bodies other than the government could play a vital role, too. Donations from the private sector (such as banks or insurance companies) as well as support from the region could be effectively used to implement this task.

3.2.5 Consulting communities

The laws as such were, however, the subjects of intense discussion and some of the contents were felt to neglect people's needs and their values and beliefs. These negative attitudes referred not only to the process of making laws but also to the dissemination of information on the new laws afterwards. The first was felt to be carried out by only a few privileged people in town while the second, consequently, utilised communication means that were only available in urban areas.

Future information dissemination activities should therefore utilise communication means that are accessible for the majority of the population, that is, road shows and radio. But the dissemination exercise would not be such a problem if people were aware of the exercise - preferably by having participated in the making of new laws.

3.3 Informal support groups

A large number of, especially, female participants were triggered to inquire about co-operatives and support groups. This referred mainly to the process of establishing a new group in their area, where, so they reported, no other group, which they could join, had been present. Information on how to form such a group, in order to organise themselves, to provide each other with support and advice and to gain an income if forces are joined, was requested frequently. Weekly meetings with different topics, and knowledgeable speakers from other groups in the area, to support learning and information exchange, were suggested.

Often, it was mentioned that the stress women and men go through after the death of a partner is extremely unbearable and social expectations people in their communities have of widows or widowers can be tough to live with. If, in this situation, no one assists the person with sensible advice, espe-

166

cially women can lose hope and give in to the nearest option such as widow inheritance or prostitution. Many people mentioned the strong need for effective psychological counselling to cope with loss and to refocus priorities in their lives. It extended to specific counselling on HIV/AIDS issues. This counselling, so it was stated, should give women the confidence to resist pressures from their social environment.

3.4 The way forward

The aim of this study was to contribute to the current empowerment discussion in the nonformal educational field, and to explore alternative methods of strengthening the position of women and communities. While it is acknowledged that attitudes and practices do take time to change, it is anticipated that this process could be supported by more studies in the field of communication and education research in the near future. These studies could allow further insights into beneficiaries' needs and will lead to the planning and implementation of effective programmes to address those needs.

It is a hope that final choices and decisions concerning strategies and programmes will, one day, be left with those who are most affected by the consequences of these decisions. Facilitating access to any kind of information for any kind of target group should therefore have priority in order to enable people to make their own informed decisions. Video, it is hoped, should be a favoured alternative tool in adult education and a qualitative method of further research that looks into ways of strengthening the status of women and empowering its beneficiaries to make informed choices throughout their lives.

Literature and Appendices

1 Literature

Adams, Maurianne 1997: Pedagogical frameworks for social justice education. In: Maurianne Adams; Lee Anne Bell; Pat Griffin (Eds.) 1997: Teaching for diversity and social justice. A sourcebook. New York; London: Routledge. 30-43.

Adult Literacy Organisation of Zimbabwe (ALOZ) 1998: Report of the Adult Literacy Tutors refresher course. Domboshawa National Training Centre 17-21 August 1998. Unpublished.

Aggleton, Peter; Parker, Richard 2002: World AIDS Campaign 2002-2003. A conceptual framework and basis for action: HIV/AIDS Stigma and discrimination. Geneva: UNAIDS.

Aggleton, Peter; Rivers, Kim 1999: Adolescent sexuality, gender and the HIV pandemic. Thomas Coram Research Unit of the Institute of Education of the University of London. New York: UNDP HIV and Development Programme.

Agimbe, Christine; Butegwa, Florence; Osakue, Grace; Nduna, Sydia 1994: Legal rights awareness among women in Africa. Harare: WILDAF.

Ajzen, Icek 1993: Attitude theory and the attitude relation. In: Dagmar Krebs; Peter Schmidt (Eds.) 1993: New directions in attitude measurement. Berlin/New York: Walter de Gruyter. 41-55.

Ajzen, Icek; Fishbein, M. 1980: Understanding attitudes and predicting social behaviour. New York: Prentice Hall.

Anyaegbunam, Chike; Mefalopulos, Paolo; Moetsabi, Titus 1998: Participatory Rural Communication Appraisal. Starting with the people. An action programme resource. Harare: SADC Centre of Communication for development/Rome: Food and Agriculture Organisation of the United Nations.

Armstrong, Alice 1995: Law and women's development: An introduction. In: Welshman Ncube; Julie Stewart (Eds.) 1995: Widowhood, inheritance laws, customs and practices in Southern Africa. Harare: WLSA. 7-13.

Armstrong, Alice; Beyani, Chaloka; Himonga, Chuma; Kabeberi-Macharia, Janet; Molokomme, Athalia; Ncube, Welshman; Nhlapo, Thandabantu; Rwezaura, Bart; Stewart, Julie 1993: Uncovering reality. Excavating women's rights in African Family Law. Working Paper No. 7. Harare: WLSA.

Aufderheide, Pat 2002: NGOs, Funders, and Filmmakers: Jointly Crafting Tools for Social Action Agendas. Paper presented at the Our Media Not Theirs II Preconference on Alternative Media. Barcelona: IAMCR.

Baacke, Dieter 1994: Massenmedien. In: Rudolf Tippelt (Hrsg.) 1994: Handbuch der Erwachsenenbildung/Weiterbildung. Opladen: Leske+Budrich. 455-62.

------1995: Zum pädagogischen Widerwillen gegen den Seh-Sinn. In: Dieter Baacke; Franz Josef Roell (Hrsg.) 1995: Weltbilder, Wahrnehmung, Wirklichkeit. Bildung als ästhetischer Lernprozeß. Opladen: Leske+Budrich. 25-49.

Bandura, Albert 1977: Social learning theory. New Jersey: Prentice Hall.

------1986: Social foundation of thought and action. A social cognitive theory. Englewood Cliffs, New Jersey: Prentice Hall.

------1995: Exercise of personal and collective efficacy in changing societies. In: Albert Bandura (Ed.) 1995: Self-efficacy in changing societies. New York: Cambridge University Press. 1-45.

------2001: Social cognitive theory of mass communication. In: Media Psychology, 3. 265-298.

Batezat, Elinor; Mwalo, Margaret 1989: Women in Zimbabwe. Harare: SAPES Trust.

Bell, Lee Anne 1997: Theoretical foundations for social justice education. In: Maurianne Adams; Lee Anne Bell; Pat Griffin (Eds.) 1997: Teaching for diversity and social justice. A sourcebook. New York; London: Routledge. 3-15.

Bohner, Gerd; Waenke, Michaela 2002: Attitudes and attitude change. Hove: Psychology Press.

Bookman, Anne; Morgen, Sandra 1988: Rethinking women and politics. An introductory essay. In: Anne Bookman; Sandra Morgen (Eds.) 1988: Women and the politics of empowerment. Philadelphia: Temple University Press. 3-29.

Bourdillion, M.F.C. 1975: Is Customary Law customary? In: NADA Vol. XI, No 2. 140-149.

Cabernero-Verzosa, Cecilia 1996: Communication for Behaviour Change. Washington D.C.: The World Bank.

Chakanetsa, Charity 1992: In testate succession of the matri-estate today - a case study of the current problem. In: Julie Stewart (Ed.) 1992: Inheritance in Zimbabwe. WLSA Paper No. 6. June 1992. Harare: WLSA. 88-100.

Chikambi, Petronilla 1992: A look at Zimbabwe's movie industry. In: Look and Listen, Vol. 27/6 July - 19 July. 6.

Chinhema, Ruth 1999: Widowed mother jailed after son attempts to have her evicted from home. In: The Herald, November 19, 1999. 1.

Chiumbu, Sarah Helen 1997: Democracy, human rights and the media. IMK report no. 23. Oslo: University of Oslo.

Clarke, Roy 2001: Women empowerment framework. In: Nigel Hall; Werner Mauch (Eds.) 2001: Gender and HIV/AIDS. A report of the International Workshop on the Development of Empowering Educational HIV/AIDS Prevention Strategies and Gender Sensitive Materials held in Nairobi, Kenya, 9-13 July, 2001. Hamburg: Unesco Institute for Education; Harare: SAfAIDS. 24-25.

170

Colverson, Kathleen E. 1999: Women in agriculture: participation and access. In: Shirley A. White (Ed.) 1999: The art of facilitating participation. Releasing the power of grassroots communication. New Delhi; Thousand Oaks; London: Sage Publications. 160-174.

Coombs, Philip H.; Ahmed, Manzoor 1974: Attacking rural poverty. How nonformal education can help. Baltimore: The John Hopkins University Press.

Daily News Reporter 2003: Local women step up to fight for their rights. In: The Daily News, Saturday 8 March 2003. 17.

De Bruyn, Maria 1995: Introduction: A gender-based approach to advancing women's social status and position. In: Maria De Bruyn (Ed.) 1995: Advancing women's status: Gender, society and development. Amsterdam: Royal Tropical Institute. 11-20.

De Fossard, Esther (Ed.) 1996: How to write a radio serial drama for social development. A script writer's manual. Centre for communication programs. Baltimore: The John Hopkins University School of Public Health.

Dengu-Zvobgo, Kebokile; Donzwa, Beatrice Rose; Gwaunza, Elizabeth Chiedza; Kazembe, Joyce Laetitia; Ncube, Welshman; Stewart, Julie E. 1994: Inheritance in Zimbabwe. Law, customs and practices. Harare: WLSA.

Dighe, Anita 1995: Women's literacy and empowerment: The Nellore experience. In: Carolyn Medel-Anonuevo (Ed.) 1995: Women, education and empowerment: Pathways towards autonomy. UIE Studies No. 5. Hamburg: Unesco Institute for Education. 39-45.

Donzwa, Beatrice; Ncube, Welshman; Stewart, Julie 1995: Which law? What law? Playing with the rules. In: Welshman Ncube; Julie Stewart (Eds.) 1995: Widowhood, inheritance laws, customs and practices in Southern Africa. Harare: WLSA. 73-107.

Durt, Mariana 1992: Bildungspolitik in Zimbabwe 1899-1990. Vom „Industrial Training" zu „Education with Production". Erfahrungen mit einem praxis-orientierten Bildungskonzept. Frankfurt: Verlag für interkulturelle Kommunikation.

Eagly, A.H.; Chaiken, S. 1993: The psychology of attitudes. San Diego, CA: Harcourt Brace Jovanovich.

Easton, Peter A. 1997: Sharpening our tools. Improving evaluation in adult and nonformal education. UIE Studies 4, 1997. UNESCO Institute for Education/DSE. Hamburg: UIE.

Enochs, Liz 1992: Where there's a will. In: Horizon, June 1992. 37.

Experiential Momentum 2002: The Wills and Inheritance Laws Programme Report for the International Video Fair and Media for Development Trust. Harare. Unpublished.

Fetterman, David (Ed.) 1994: Qualitative approach to evaluation in education. The silent scientific revolution. New York/Westport, Connecticut/London: Praeger.

171

Food and Agriculture Organisation of the United Nations (FAO) 1990: Powerful images. Planning, production and user's guide. Rome: FAO.

------ 1998: Communication for development. Knowledge and information for food security in Africa: From traditional media to the Internet. Rome: FAO.

Freire, Paulo 1973: Pädagogik der Unterdrückten. Bildung als Praxis der Freiheit. Reinbek: Rowohlt.

Friebertshaeuser, Barbara; Prengel, Annedore (Hg.) 1997: Handbuch qualitative Forschungsmethoden in der Erziehungswissenschaft. Weinheim, München: Juventa Verlag.

Gaceru, Gethiga 1994: A widow's nightmare. In: The Standard, April 24, 1994. 6.

Gacheru, wa Margaretta 1994: Neria: the 'new' African woman. In: Daily Nation, April 22, 1994. 4.

Getecha, Ciru; Chipika, Jesimen (Eds.) 1995: Zimbabwe women's voices. Harare: ZWRCN.

Ghosh, Akhila 1984: Media and rural women. In: Kamla Bhasin; Bina Agarwal (Eds.) 1984: Women and media. Analysis, alternatives and action. Rome: ISIS International. 63-68.

Glaser, Barney; Strauss, Anselm 1967: The discovery of grounded theory: strategies for qualitative research. New York: De Gruyter.

Gokova, Johnah 1997: Community intervention strategies on gender. In: Musasa Project 1997: Violence against women in Zimbabwe: Strategies for action. Harare: Musasa Project. 42-43.

Gordon, Rosemary 1998: 'Girls cannot think as boys do'. In: Caroline Sweetman (Ed.) 1998: Gender, education and training. Oxford: Oxfam. 53-58.

Government of Zimbabwe 1999: Working document for National AIDS Council. National HIV/AIDS strategic frame work for a national response to HIV/AIDS 2000-2004. Harare: The Government Printer.

Gumbo, Perpetua 1998: The gender dimension in social security: a historical perspective. In: Edwin Kaseke (Ed.) 1998: Social security systems in rural Zimbabwe. Harare: Friedrich-Ebert-Foundation. 15-22.

Gwaunza, Elisabeth C. 1995: Women, Law and Democracy. The position of women and children in Zimbabwe. In: J. Balch; D. Cammack; P. Johnson; R. Morgan (Eds.) 1995: Transcending the legacy. Children in the new Southern Africa. Amsterdam; Harare; Nairobi: AEI; SARDC; UNICEF. 178-187.

Hall, Nigel; Mauch, Werner 2001: Gender and HIV/AIDS. A report of the International Workshop on the Development of Empowering Educational HIV/AIDS Prevention Strategies and Gender Sensitive Materials held in Nairobi, Kenya, 9-13 July, 2001. Hamburg: Unesco Institute for Education; Harare: SAfAIDS.

Hamilton-Wray, Tama Lynne 1992: The cultural shareability of edutainment media in global Africa: an explorative study. Ohio. Unpublished.

172

Hausmann, Christine 1998: Nonformal education for women in Zimbabwe. Empowerment strategies and status improvement. European university studies: Series 11, Education, Vol. 751. Frankfurt a. Main; Berlin; Bern; New York; Paris; Vienna: Peter Lang GmbH.

------1999: She dared to fight back. A study on the qualitative impact of *Neria*. Harare: Media for Development Trust. Unpublished.

------2001: Neria support manual. Harare: Media for Development Trust.

Heise, Lori 1989: Crimes of gender. In: World Watch, March, April 1989. 12-21.

Herald Reporter, The 2002: Double tragedy for Chitungwiza widower. In: The Herald, April 26, 2002. 2.

Hill, Heather 1993: The widow's revenge. In: Africa Report. March, April 1993. 64-66.

Hochheimer, John L. 1999: Planning community radio as participatory development. In: Shirley A. White (Ed.) 1999: The art of facilitating participation. Releasing the power of grassroots communication. New Delhi; Thousand Oaks; London: Sage Publications. 245-258.

Horton, D.; Wohl, R. R. (1956). Mass communication as parasocial interaction: Observations on intimacy at a distance. In: Psychiatry, 19. 215-229.

Hove, Chenjerai 1998: Was there ever human rights in Zimbabwean culture? In: Woman Plus Volume 3, Number 2, May-July 1998. 12-13.

Hudock, Ann C. 1993: The impact of social message videos in Africa: Results of a rapid assessment evaluation. Columbia. Unpublished.

Jirira, Kwanele Ona 1995: Gender, politics and democracy: Kuvaka Patsva (Reconstructing) - The discourse. In: SAFERE – Southern African Feminist Review. Gender, politics and democracy. Vol. 1, No. 2. Harare: SAPES Trust Books. 1-29.

Jongepier, Maaike; Appel, Marguerite 1995: A critical review of education and training. In: Maria De Bruyn (Ed.) 1995: Advancing women's status: Gender, society and development. Amsterdam: Royal Tropical Institute. 60-74.

K2 Techtop Consult 2001: Baseline survey on the level of national awareness, knowledge, attitudes and practices on wills and inheritance matters. Harare. Unpublished.

Kapambwe, Thandi 2000: Widowers are not expected to show grief. In: The Daily News, September 6, 2000. 24-26.

Karikoga, Masimba 1999: Film industry plunged into financial 'blackout'. In: The Herald, August 4, 1999. 5.

------ 2001: Film *Neria* dubbed into Shona, Ndebele versions. In: The Herald, September 29, 2001. 8.

Karisa, Portia 2003: Lobola being abused. In: The Herald, January 12, 2003. 11.

Karl, Marilee 1995: Women and empowerment. Participation and decision-making. London; New Jersey: Zed Books Ltd.

Kaseke, Edwin 1995: Structural adjustment and protection of the poor: The 'Social Welfare Component' of the 'Social Development Fund' in Zimbabwe. In: J. Balch; D. Cammack; P. Johnson; R. Morgan (Eds.) 1995: Transcending the legacy. Children in the new Southern Africa.: Amsterdam; Harare; Nairobi: AEI; SARDC; UNICEF. 191-199.

------ (Ed.) 1998: Social security systems in rural Zimbabwe. Harare: Friedrich-Ebert-Foundation.

Kempley, Rita 1993: 'Neria': Laws and change in Zimbabwe. In: The Washington Post, April 9, 1993. 7.

Kiiti, Ndunge; Nielsen, Eric 1999: Facilitator or advocate: What's the difference? In: Shirley A. White (Ed.) 1999: The art of facilitating participation. Releasing the power of grassroots communication. New Delhi; Thousand Oaks; London: Sage Publications. 52-67.

Kincaid, Lawrence D.; Schramm, Wilbur 1996: Fundamental human communication. A professional development module. Harare, Baltimore: USAID; ZNFPC; JHU, CCP.

Koniz-Booher, Peggy 1999: Confessions of an outside facilitator: Developing educational materials in the Dominican Republic. In: Shirley A. White (Ed.) 1999: The art of facilitating participation. Releasing the power of grassroots communication. New Delhi; Thousand Oaks; London: Sage Publications. 92-120.

Kriger, Norma J. 1992: Zimbabwe's Guerrilla war. Peasant voices. Cambridge: University Press.

Kumar, Krishna 1987: Rapid, low-cost data collection methods for A.I.D. AID program design and evaluation methodology report No. 10. Unpublished.

Lenhart, Volker 1993: „Bildung für alle". Zur Bildungskrise. in der Dritten Welt. Darmstadt: Wissenschaftliche Buchgesellschaft.

Lind, Agneta; Johnston, Anton 1990: Adult literacy in the Third World. A review of objectives and strategies. Stockholm: Sida.

Longwe, Sara Hlupekile 1998: Education for women's empowerment or schooling for women's subordination? In: Caroline Sweetman (Ed.) 1998: Gender, education and training. Oxford: Oxfam. 19-26.

Manyemba, Eunice 1993: Spouses' rights to inherit property may be extended. In: The Herald, March 29, 1993. 1-3.

Mararike, Claude 1995: Grassroots leadership - the process of rural development in Zimbabwe. Harare: UZ Publications.

Maruma, Olley 1993: The role of the filmmaker in Southern Africa. In: Keith Shiri (Ed.) 1993: Africa at the pictures. London: National Film Theatre. 51-58.

Matewa, Chido E.F. 2002: Media and the Empowerment of Communities for Social Change. A thesis submitted to the University of Manchester for the degree of PhD in the Faculty of Education. Unpublished.

174

Matope, Tsitsi 2002: Wrangle over deceased businesswoman's estate. In: The Herald, May 22, 2002. 2.

Matsikidze, Cecilia; Mawuru, Godwin 1989: Analysis of the focus group discussions. Harare. Unpublished.

May, Joan 1983: Zimbabwean women in customary and colonial law. Zambeziana Vol. XIV. Gweru; Harare; Masvingo: Mambo Press.

Mbiti, John S. 1974: Afrikanische Religion und Weltanschauung. Berlin; New York: Walter de Gruyter.

Mc Fadden, Patricia 1997: Issues of power and contestation in the Women's Movement. In: Woman Plus, May-August 1997. 26-29.

Mc Guire, W.J. (1989). Theoretical foundations of campaigns. In: R.E. Rice & C.K. Atkin (Eds.) 1989: Public communication campaigns. Newbury Park, C.A.: Sage.

Mc Quail, Denis 1987: Mass communication theory. An introduction. London, Thousand Oaks, New Delhi: Sage Publications.

Meyns, Peter 1999: Simbabwe am Ende der Ära Mugabe - Nationale Probleme und regionale Konflikte. In: Aus Politik und Zeitgeschichte. Beilage zur Wochenzeitung ‚Das Parlament'. B 27/99. 2. Juli 1999. 30-39.

Moemeka, Andrew Azukaego 1997: Communalistic societies. Community and self-respect as African values. In: Clifford Christians; Michael Traber (Eds.) 1997: Communication ethics and universal values. Thousand Oaks; London; New Delhi: Sage Publications. 170-193.

Moetsabi, Titus 2001: Communication strategy. Community dialogue, collective actions - making an impact. Harare. Unpublished.

Monaco, James 1981: How to read a film. The art, technology, language, history and theory of film and media. New York; Oxford: Oxford University Press.

Moyo, Peter 2001: Updated version of Neria out soon. In: The Standard, April 29, 2001. 7.

Mukunoweshuro, Enes 1992: Some good news mixed with some not so good news. In: Julie Stewart (Ed.) 1992: Inheritance in Zimbabwe. WLSA Paper No. 6. June 1992. Harare: WLSA. 70-87.

Murphy, Josette 1995: Gender issues in World Bank lending. Washington D.C.: The World Bank.

Musasa Project 1997: Violence against women in Midlands: Strategies for action. Harare: Musasa Project.

Muzondo, Noel 1999: Magaya: The symbol of resistance. In: Speak out; Taurai; Khulumani. Issue No. 48, August-October 1999. 5.

Ncube, Welshman 1998: Re-evaluating law, tradition, custom and practice. Custody and access to non-marital children in Zimbabwe. In: Welshman Ncube (Ed.) 1998: Law, culture, tradition and children's rights in Eastern and Southern Africa. Ashgate: Dartmouth Publishing Company Ltd. Aldershot. 150-181.

175

Ncube, Welshman; Stewart, Julie E.; Dengu-Zvobgo, Kebokile C.; Donzwa, Beatrice R.; Gwaunza, Elizabeth C.; Kazembe, Joyce, L.; Nzira, Tsitsi G. 1997: Paradigms of exclusion: Women's access to resources in Zimbabwe. Harare: WLSA.

Nestvogel, Renate 1985: Women in Zimbabwe. The patriarchal system and its historical development. Arbeitsmaterialien für den landeskundlichen Unterricht. Heft 5. Bonn: DSE.

Office of the High Commissioner for Human Rights (OHCHR) 1997: Basic information kit No 2. New York; Geneva: UN.

Owen, Margaret 1996: A world of widows. London, New Jersey: Zed Books.

Papa, Michael J.; Auwal, Mohammad A.; Singhal, Arvind 1995: Dialectic of Control and Emancipation in Organising for Social Change: A Multi-theoretic Study of the Grameen Bank. In: Communication Theory, 5(3). 189-223.

------ 1997: Organising for Social Change Within Concertive Control Systems: Member Identification, Empowerment, and the Masking of Discipline. In: Communication Monographs, 64. 1-31.

Papa, Michael J.; Singhal, Arvind; Ghanekar, D.V.; Papa, Wendy H. 2000: Organizing for Social Change Through Co-operative Action: The [Dis]Empowering Dimensions of Women's Communication. In: Communication Theory, 10 (1). 90-123.

Papa, Michael J.; Singhal, Arvind; Law, Sweety; Pant, Saumya; Sood, Suruchi; Rogers, Everett M.; Shefner-Rogers, Corinne 2000: Entertainment-Education and Social Change: An Analysis of Parasocial Interaction, Social Learning, Collective Efficacy, and Paradoxical Communication. In: Journal of Communication, 50 (4). 31-55.

Petty, R. E.; Cacioppo, J. T. 1981: Attitudes and persuasion: Classic and contemporary approaches. Dubuque, IA: Wm. C. Brown Company.

------ 1986: Communication and persuasion: central and peripheral routes to attitude change. New York: Springer.

Pfeiffer, Wolfgang 1993: Der Film in Simbabwe und seine Produktionsbedingungen. In: Haus der Kulturen der Welt 1993: Filmwelt Afrika. Berlin: Haus der Kulturen der Welt. 61-64.

Piotrow, Phyllis Tilson; Kincaid, Lawrence D.; Rimon, Jose G II; Rinehart, Ward 1997: Health Communication - Lessons from Family Planning and Reproductive Health. Baltimore: Johns Hopkins School of Public Health, Center for Communication Programmes.

Prochaska, J.O.; DiClemente, C.C.; Norcoss, J. C. 1992: In search of how people change: Applications to addictive behaviours. In: American Psychologist 47:1992. 1102-1114.

Ramirez, Ricardo 1999: A journey in search of facilitative communication. In: Shirley A. White (Ed.) 1999: The art of facilitating participation. Releasing the power of

176

grassroots communication. New Delhi; Thousand Oaks; London: Sage Publications. 80-91.

Reimann, Cordula 2000: Konfliktbearbeitung in Theorie und Praxis: Spielt „Gender" eine Rolle? AFB-Texte Nr. 1, März 2000.

Riber, John & staff writers 1993: Distribution of African films in Africa, based on the Neria experience. In: Africa Film and TV 1993. Harare: Z Promotions Pvt. Ltd. 17-19.

Riber, John 2001: Overview of the Audio-visual Scene in Zimbabwe - June 2001. Unpublished.

Riber, Louise 1992: *Neria* film-script. Harare. Unpublished.

Rimon, Jose G. II 2002: HIV/AIDS and behaviour change communication. Edited transcript of a verbal presentation published by the Integration magazine. From the Communication initiative web site www.comminit.com\hotfive_joserimon.htm.

Rockefeller Foundation, Communication and Social Change Network 2001: Measuring and Evaluating Communication for Social Change. www.comminit.com.

Rogers, Everett 1995: The diffusion of innovations. New York: The Free Press.

RSC Zimbabwe 2001: RSC report. Wills and Inheritance Laws Program. Harare. Unpublished.

Runganga, Agnes O.; Sundby, Johanne; Aggleton, Peter 2001: Culture, identity and reproductive failure in Zimbabwe. In: Sexualities Vol. 4(3). London, Thousand Oaks, CA and New Delhi: SAGE Publications. 315-332.

Ruzvidzo, Thokozile; Tichagwa, Wilfred 2001: Report on the participatory rural and urban communication appraisal of awareness, knowledge, attitude and practice in relation to wills and inheritance. Harare. Unpublished.

Schmidt, Bettina 1991: Simbabwe: Die Entstehung einer Nation. Sozialwissenschaftliche Studien zu internationalen Problemen. Bd. 154. Saarbrücken, Fort Lauderdale: Verlag breitenbach publishers.

Schmidt, Elizabeth 1992: Peasants, traders and wives. Shona women in the history of Zimbabwe (1870-1939). Portsmouth: Heinemann; Harare: Baobab, London: James Currey.

Schwarzkopf, Dietrich 1989: Fernsehen und Meinungsbildung. In: Ruprecht Kurzrock (Hg.)1989: Medienforschung. Schriftenreihe der Rias Funkuniversität. Berlin: Colloquium Verlag. 44-52.

Scrampickal, Jacob 1994: Voice to the voiceless. The power of people's theatre in India. New Delhi: Manohar.

Shenje, A. 1992: The forgotten victims? African widows and their use of the provisions of the Deceased Persons Family Maintenance Act. In: Julie Stewart (Ed.) 1992: Inheritance in Zimbabwe. WLSA Paper No. 6. June 1992. Harare: WLSA. 53-69.

Siegelaub, Seth 1979: Preface: a communication on communication. In: Armand Mattelart; Seth Siegelaub (Eds.) 1979: Communication and class struggle. 1. Capital-

177

ism, imperialism. New York: International General; Bagnolet: International mass media research centre. 11-21.

Singhal, Arvind; Rogers, Everett M. 2002: A Theoretical Agenda for Entertainment-Education. In: Communication Theory, 12 (2). 117-135.

Smith, Arlinda 1993: She dared to fight back... In: Every Wednesday, March 31, 1993. 27.

St. Anne, Simone 1999: Synergising participation: Are you able to enable? In: Shirley A. White (Ed.) 1999: The art of facilitating participation. Releasing the power of grassroots communication. New Delhi; Thousand Oaks; London: Sage Publications. 68-79.

Stahlberg, Dagmar; Frey, Dieter 1996: Attitudes: Structure, measurement and functions. In: Miles Hewstone; Wolfgang Stroebe; Geoffrey M. Stepfenson (Eds.) 1996: Introduction to social psychology. A European perspective. Oxford; Blackwell Publishers. 206-239.

Stein, Jane 1997: Empowerment and women's health - Theory, methods and practice. London, New Jersey: ZED Books.

Stewart, Julie; Tsanga, Amy 2001: Law, literature, materials, organisations and methods: Inventory and review. Harare. Unpublished.

Storey, John 1996: Radio serial drama: the theory behind the practice. In: Esther De Fossard (Ed.) 1996: How to write a radio serial drama for social development. A script writer's manual. Center for communication programs. Baltimore: The John Hopkins University School of Public Health. XI-XIX.

Stroebe, Wolfgang; Jonas, Klaus 1996: Principles of attitude formation and strategies of change. In: Miles Hewstone; Wolfgang Stroebe; Geoffrey M. Stepfenson (Eds.) 1996: Introduction to social psychology. A European perspective. Oxford: Blackwell Publishers. 241-275.

Stromquist, Nelly 1993: Praktische und theoretische Grundlagen für Empowerment. In: Nord-Süd aktuell, 2/93. 259-266.

------ 1995: The theoretical and practical bases for empowerment. In: Carolyn Medel-Anonuevo (Ed.) 1995: Pathways towards autonomy. Women, education and empowerment UIE studies 5. Hamburg: Unesco Institute for Education. 13-22.

------ 1997: Literacy practices among adult women: An attempt at critical conceptualisation. In: Carolyn Medel-Anonuevo (Ed.) 1997: Negotiating and creating spaces of power. Women's educational practices amidst crises. UIE Studies No. 7. Hamburg: Unesco Institute for Education. 25-31.

------ 1999: By way of introduction to Workshop 1. In: Carolyn Medel-Anonuevo (Ed.) 1999: Learning gender justice through women's discourses. Report of Theme IV of the Fifth International Conference on Adult Education. Hamburg: Unesco Institute for Education. 5-6.

Tsanga, Amy S. 1998: Taking law to the people: the experience of Zimbabwe. Unpublished PhD thesis.

United Nations Children's Fund (UNICEF) 1994: Children and women in Zimbabwe. A situation analysis. Update 1994. Harare: UNICEF.

United Nations Development Programme (UNDP) 1998a: Human Development Report 1998. Zimbabwe. New York/Oxford: Oxford University Press.

------ 1998b Overcoming human poverty. The UNDP Poverty Report. New York: UNDP.

------ 2002 The Human Development Report 2002. New York/Oxford: Oxford University Press.

United Nations Educational, Scientific and cultural organisation (UNESCO) 2002a: Guidelines for preparing gender responsive EFA plans. Bangkok: UNESCO Asia and Pacific Regional Bureau for Education.

------ 2002b: Education for all. Is the world on track? EFA Global monitoring report 2002. Paris: UNESCO.

United Nations Population Fund (UNFPA) 1995: A new role for men - partners for women's empowerment. New York: UNFPA.

------ 2001: Women's empowerment and reproductive health. From the UNFPA website unfpa.org/interactive population centre.

------ 2002: State of world population 2002: People, poverty and possibilities. Making development work for the poor. New York: UNFPA.

United Nations Zimbabwe Country Team (UNZCT) 1998: Zimbabwe UN common country assessment. Harare: UNIASU.

Valdez, Alejandra 1999: Enabling women's leadership in Chile. In: Carolyn Medel-Anonuevo (Ed.) 1999: Learning gender justice through women's discourses. Report of Theme IV of the Fifth International Conference on Adult Education. Hamburg: Unesco Institute for Education. 83-86.

Walker, Cherryl 1990: Women and gender in Southern Africa to 1945: An overview. In: Cherryl Walker (Ed.) 1990: Women and gender in Southern Africa to 1945. London: James Currey; Cape Town: David Philip. 1-32.

Walker, Jim 1981: The end of dialogue: Paulo Freire on politics and education. In: Robert Mackie (Ed.) 1981: Literacy and revolution. The pedagogy of Paulo Freire. New York: The Continuum. 120-150.

Weathersbee, Avis L. 1993: *Neria* probes Zimbabwe's awakening to modern culture. In: Chicago Sunday Times, Nov. 12, 1993. 26.

Weis Bentzon, Agnete; Hellum, Anne; Stewart, Julie; Ncube, Welshman; Agersnap, Torben 1998: Pursuing grounded theory in law. South-North experiences in developing women's law. Harare: Mond Books; Oslo: Tano Aschehoug.

Weiss, Ruth 1985: Die Frauen von Simbabwe. München: Frauenbuchverlag.

------ 1990: Mbuya Mudzi und die Mütter: 10 Jahre danach. In: Heike Kammerer-Grothaus (Ed.) 1990: 10 Jahre Simbabwe: Kunst und Geschichte. Bremen: Übersee Museum. 115-116.

White, Shirley A.; Nair, K. Sadanandan 1999: The catalyst communicator: facilitation without fear. In: Shirley A. White (Ed.) 1999: The art of facilitating participation. Releasing the power of grassroots communication. New Delhi; Thousand Oaks; London: Sage Publications. 35-51.

Women in Law and Development in Southern Africa (WILDAF) 1993: Draft programme of activities for the national inheritance campaign by WILDAF and its member organisations in Zimbabwe. Harare. Unpublished.

Women in Law in Southern Africa (WLSA) 2002: The Wills and Inheritance Laws Programme Information Kit. Harare: WLSA.

Wray, Richard J. 1991: Taking stock of Consequences: The evaluation of a dramatic film about teenage pregnancy in an educational setting in Kenya. Unpublished.

Young, I. M. 1994: Punishment, treatment, empowerment: Three approaches to policy for pregnant addicts. In: Feminist Studies, 20. 33-57.

Zambia Association for research and development (ZARD) 1996: Zambia today: a gender perspective. Analysis of the public views. Lusaka: ZARD.

Zigomo, Lydia 1998: Do we have a culture of Human Rights in Zimbabwe? In: Woman Plus, Volume 3, Number 2 May-July 1998. 3-5.

Zimbabwe Women's Resource Centre and Network (ZWRCN) 1999: Women and the Zimbabwean Constitution. Fact Sheets. Harare: ZWRCN.

Zimbardo, Philip G.; Leippe, Michael R. 1991: The psychology of attitude change and social influence. Philadelphia: Temple University Press.

2 Appendices

2.1 Participants' residential areas – provinces

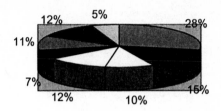

2.2 Participants' residential areas – rural/urban

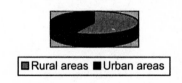

2.3   Questionnaire form Road show/Ladies' Clubs (English version)

A.

Date of screen-ing; venue	Audience type; numbers	Materials used; language	Results ob-served	Recommendations

B.

Use of the training package

Which materials were used how? (feature film/support video/support manual in which language, order, manner)

Appropriateness of the support package for the circumstances

Was there enough time to discuss relevant sections of the support video/manual? How far were questions suitable to obtain your goals? Did the style of the materials reach your target group? How?

Organisations /institutions recommendations on training materials production

C.

What was the viewers understanding of inheritance, inheritance laws and making a will before watching the film?

How did they change as a result of watching the film?

What did they understand and what messages did they get?

What systems exist for solving problems related to widow inheritance and property grabbing? In the community?

Could this change in nature, scope or quality?

Which intended messages of the film were not recognised or understood by the viewer?

State the participants view on the media used (film instead of radio, brochures, books, talks).

Did this influence the way information was received? How?

Do participants derive lessons from the film? If so which?

How will this change or has this changed the situation for widows and widowers? Community support? Other comments

IKO - Verlag für Interkulturelle Kommunikation

Holger Ehling Publishing • Edition ZeitReise • Edition Hipparchia • Edition ÖKOglobal

Frankfurt am Main • London

Büro Frankfurt am Main	Internet: www.iko-verlag.de	Büro London
Postfach 90 04 21; D-60444 Frankfurt am Main	Verkehrs-Nr.: 10896	70 c, Wrentham Avenue
Assenheimerstr. 17, D–60489 Frankfurt	Auslieferung: info@suedost-verlags-service.de	London NW10 3HG, UK
Tel.: +49-(0)69-78 48 08		Phone: +44-(0)20-76881688
Fax: +49-(0)69-78 96 575		Fax: +44-(0)20-76881699
e-mail: info@iko-verlag.de		

Aus dem Verlagsprogramm

Claudia Lohrenscheit
Das Recht auf Menschenrechtsbildung –
Grundlagen und Ansätze einer Pädagogik
der Menschenrechte
Mit einer Studie über aktuelle Entwicklungs-
linien der „Human Rights Education" in Süd-
afrika
Internationale Beiträge zu Kindheit, Jugend,
Arbeit und Bildung, Bd. 10
2004, 332 S., € 21,90, ISBN 3-88939-718-2

Gregor Lang-Wojtasik/
Claudia Lohrenscheit (Hrsg.)
Entwicklungspädagogik –
Globales Lernen –
Internationale Bildungsforschung
25 Jahre ZEP
2003, 360 S., € 24,80, ISBN 3-88939-675-5

Angelika Wehr-Koita
KOTEBA – KREIS DER SCHNECKE
Darstellung eines traditionellen afrikani-
schen Theaters als soziales Ordnungs-
system
Ein Beitrag zur interkulturellen Kommunikation in Form einer Spieltheorie
2002, 192 S., € 17,80, ISBN 3-88939-647-X

Wolfgang Broszat
Einsatz von Druckmaterialien zur
Fortbildung von Kleinbauern in
Entwicklungsländern
2000, 172 S., € 18,00, ISBN 3-88939-529-5

Ulrike Wiegelmann (Hrsg.)
Afrikanisch – europäisch – islamisch?
Entwicklungsdynamik des Erziehungs-
wesens in Senegal
Historisch-vergleichende Sozialisations- und
Bildungsforschung, Band 5
2002, 486 S., € 22,80, ISBN 3-88939-625-9

Asit Datta/Gregor Lang-Wojtasik (Hrsg.)
Bildung zur Eigenständigkeit
Vergessene reformpädagogische Ansätze
aus vier Kontinenten
Historisch-vergleichende Sozialisations- und
Bildungsforschung, Band 6
2002, 304 S., € 24,80, ISBN 3-88939-644-5

Erika Schmidt/Milena Vogt
„Abantwana Benkosi – Königskinder"
Township Theatre in Zimbabwe und Versu-
che zimbabwisch-deutscher Theaterarbeit
2000, 348 S., € 29,80, ISBN 3-88939-538-4

Werner Trieselmann
Fernsehen in der Kultur der Igbo
Eine medienethnologische Untersuchung
am Beispiel der Nri in Südostnigeria,
Westafrika
Göttinger Kulturwissenschaftliche Schriften,
Band 10
1999, 366 S., € 32,80, ISBN 3-88939-504-X

Bestellen Sie bitte über den Buchhandel oder direkt beim Verlag.
Wir senden Ihnen gerne unser Titelverzeichnis zu.